DATE DUE

RIVERSIDE COMMUNITY COLLEGE
LIBRARY
Riverside, California

THE MORTAL DANGER

Aleksandr I. Solzhenitsyn

THE MORTAL
DANGER

HOW MISCONCEPTIONS ABOUT RUSSIA
IMPERIL AMERICA

Second Edition

TRANSLATED FROM THE RUSSIAN BY
Michael Nicholson and Alexis Klimoff

HARPER TORCHBOOKS
Harper & Row, Publishers, New York
Cambridge, Philadelphia, San Francisco, Washington
London, Mexico City, São Paulo, Singapore, Sydney

The Mortal Danger was originally published in *Foreign Affairs,* Vol. 58, No. 4 (Spring 1980), under the title "Misconceptions about Russia Are a Threat to America." The translation has been slightly revised for the present edition. Letters from Robert C. Tucker and Silvio J. Treves were originally published in *Foreign Affairs,* Vol. 58, No. 5 (Summer 1980). Letters from Robert W. Thurston, Eugen Loebl, John R. Dunlap, and Alexander Dallin, and Aleksandr I. Solzhenitsyn's "The Courage to See" were originally published in *Foreign Affairs,* Vol. 59, No. 1 (Fall 1980).

First HARPER TORCHBOOKS edition published 1986.

LIBRARY OF CONGRESS CATALOG CARD NUMBER: 81-47087

ISBN: 0-06-132063-3

88 89 90 9 8 7 6 5

Contents

THE MORTAL DANGER

1.

Two Fallacies About Communism

Anyone not hopelessly blinded by his own illusions must recognize that the West today finds itself in a crisis, perhaps even in mortal danger. One could point to numerous particular causes or trace the specific stages over the last sixty years that have led to the present state of affairs. But the ultimate cause clearly lies in sixty years of obstinate blindness to the true nature of communism.

I am not concerned here with those who cherish, glorify, and defend communism to this day. To such people I have nothing to say. Yet there are many others who are aware that communism is an evil and a menace to the world, but who have nevertheless failed to grasp its implacable nature. And such individuals, in their capacities as policy advisers and political leaders, are even now committing fresh blunders which will inevitably have lethal repercussions in the future.

Two mistakes are especially common. One is the failure to understand the radical hostility of communism to mankind as a whole—the failure to realize that communism is irredeemable, that there exist no "better" variants of communism; that it is incapable of growing "kinder," that it cannot survive as an ideology without using terror, and that, consequently, to coexist with communism on the same planet is impossible. Either it will spread, cancer-like, to destroy mankind, or else mankind will have to rid itself of communism (and even then face lengthy treatment for secondary tumors).

The second and equally prevalent mistake is to assume an indissoluble link between the universal disease of communism and the country where it first seized control—Russia. This error skews one's perception of the threat and cripples all attempts to respond sensibly to it, thus leaving the West disarmed. This misinterpretation is fraught with tragic consequences; it is imperiling every nation, Americans no less than Russians. One will not have to await the coming of future generations to hear curses flung at those who have implanted this misapprehension in the public awareness.

I have written and spoken at length about the first of these errors, and in so doing have aroused considerable skepticism in the West, but agreement seems to be increasing with the passage of time and as the lessons of history are assimilated.

The present essay is mainly devoted to the second fallacy.

2.

Russia and the U.S.S.R.

To begin with, there is the careless and inaccurate use of the words "Russia" and "Russian" in place of "U.S.S.R." and "Soviet." (There is even a persistent emotional bias against the former: "Russian tanks have entered Prague," "Russian imperialism," "Never trust the Russians," as against "Soviet achievements in space" and "the triumphs of the Soviet ballet.") Yet it ought to be clear that these concepts are not only opposites, but are *inimical*. "Russia" is to the Soviet Union as a man is to the disease afflicting him. We do not, after all, confuse a man with his illness; we do not refer to him by the name of that illness or curse him for it. After 1917, the state as a functioning whole—the country with its government, policies, and armed forces—can no longer be referred to as Russia. It is inappropriate to apply the word "Russian" to the present authorities in the U.S.S.R., to its army, or to its future military successes and regimes of occupation throughout the world, even though the official language in each case might be Russian. (This is equally true of both China and Vietnam, only in their case no equivalent of the word "Soviet" is available.) A certain American diplomat recently exclaimed: "Let Brezhnev's Russian heart be run by an American pacemaker!" Quite wrong! He should have said "Soviet heart." Nationality is determined not by one's origins alone, but also by the direction of one's loyalties and affections. A Brezhnev who has connived at the ruin of his own people in the interests of foreign adventures has no Russian heart. All that his ilk have done—to destroy the national way of life and to pollute nature, to desecrate national shrines and monuments, and to keep the people in hunger and poverty for the last sixty years—shows that the communist leaders are alien to the people and indifferent to its suffering. (This is equally true of the ferocious Khmer Rouge, the Polish functionary who may have been reared by a Catholic mother, the young communist activist, taskmaster over a group of starving coolies, or the stolid Georges Marchais with his Kremlin-like exterior; each has turned his back on his own nationality and has embraced inhumanity.)

For present-day purposes the word "Russia" can serve only to designate an oppressed people which is denied the possibility of acting as one entity, or to denote its suppressed national consciousness, religion, and culture. Or else it can point to a future nation liberated from communism.

There was no such confusion in the 1920s when progressive Western opinion exulted over Bolshevism: the object of its enthusiasm was then named "Soviet" outright. During the tragic years of the Second World War, the concepts "Russian" and "Soviet" seem to have merged in the eyes of the world (a cruel error, which is discussed below). And with the coming of the cold war, the animosities generated were then directed principally toward the word "Russian." The effects are being felt to this day; in fact, new and bitter accusations have in recent years been leveled against all things "Russian."

3.

Ignorance Through Scholarship

The American reader receives his information about and forms his understanding of Russian history and the present-day Soviet Union chiefly from the following sources: American scholars (historians and Slavists), American diplomats, American correspondents in Moscow, and recent émigrés from the U.S.S.R. (I am not including Soviet propaganda publications, to which less credence is given lately, or the impressions of tourists, which, thanks to the skillful efforts of Intourist, remain altogether superficial.)

When American historical scholarship is confronted with the paucity of Soviet sources and with their Marxist distortion, then, for all its apparently unlimited scope and freedom from prejudice, it often unwittingly adopts the Procrustean framework provided by official Soviet historiography and, under the illusion of conducting independent research, involuntarily duplicates the approach and sometimes even the methodology of Soviet scholarship, in imitation of which it then duly skirts certain hidden and carefully hushed-up topics. It is sufficient to recall that until the most recent times the very existence of the Gulag Archipelago, its inhuman cruelty, its scope, its duration, and the sheer volume of death it generated, were not acknowledged by Western scholarship. To take a further example, the mighty outbreaks of spontaneous popular resistance to communism in our country between 1918 and 1922 have been quite disregarded by scholars in the West, and where they have been noted, they are termed "banditry," in line with Soviet parlance (for example, by Moshe Lewin).[1] In overall evaluations of Soviet history we still encounter the raptures with which "progressive" public opinion in Europe greeted the "dawning of a new life," even as the terrorism and destruction of 1917–1921 were at their height in our country. And to this day many American academics seriously refer to "the ideals of the revolution," when in fact these "ideals" manifested themselves from the very first in the murder of millions of people. Nor has Russia's distant past been spared the distorting effects of fervent radical thought in the West. In recent years American scholarship has been noticeably dominated by a most facile, one-dimensional approach, which consists in explaining the unique events of the twentieth century, first in Russia and then in other lands, not as something peculiar to communism, not as a phenomenon new to human history, but as if they derived from primordial Russian national characteristics established in some distant century. This is nothing less than a racist view. The events of the twentieth century are explained by flimsy and

[1] The reference is to Lewin's review of a book by Oliver H. Radkey, *The Unknown Civil War in Soviet Russia: A Study of the Green Movement in the Tambov Region, 1920-1921*, in *Slavic Review*, Vol. 36, No. 4 (Dec. 1977), pp. 682-683. [Tr. note]

superficial analogies drawn from the past. While communism was still the object of Western infatuation, it was hailed as the indisputable dawning of a new era. But ever since communism has had to be condemned, it has been ingeniously ascribed to the age-old Russian slave mentality.

This interpretation currently enjoys wide support, since it is so advantageous to many people: if the crimes and vices of communism are not inherent to it, but can be attributed entirely to the traditions of old Russia, then it follows that there exists no fundamental threat to the Western world; the rosy vistas of détente are preserved, together with trade and even friendship with communist countries, thereby ensuring continued comfort and security for the West; Western communists are freed from incrimination and suspicion ("they'll do a better job; theirs will be a really good communism"); and a burden falls from the conscience of those liberals and radicals who lent so much of their fervor and their assistance to this bloody regime in the past.

Scholars of this persuasion treat the history of the old Russia in a correspondingly peremptory manner. They permit themselves the most arbitrary selection of phenomena, facts, and persons, and accept unreliable or simply false versions of events. Even more striking is their almost total disregard for the spiritual history of a country that has been in existence for a thousand years, as though (as Marxists argue) this has had no bearing upon the course of its material history. It is regarded as essential when studying the history and culture of China or Thailand, or any African country, to feel some respect for the distinctive features of that culture. But when it comes to the thousand years of Eastern Christianity

in Russia, Western researchers by and large feel only astonishment and contempt: why ever did this strange world, an
entire continent, persistently reject the Western view of
things? Why did it refuse to follow the manifestly superior
path of Western society? Russia is categorically condemned
for every feature which distinguishes her from the West.

Richard Pipes's book *Russia Under the Old Regime*[2] may
stand as typical of a long series of pronouncements that dis-
tort the image of Russia. Pipes shows a complete disregard
for the spiritual life of the Russian people and its view of the
world—Christianity. He examines entire centuries of Russian history without reference to Russian Orthodoxy and its
leading proponents (suffice it to say that St. Sergius of Radonezh, whose influence upon centuries of Russian spiritual
and public life was incomparably great, is not once men-
tioned in the book, while Nil Sorsky is presented in an anec-
dotal role).[3] Thus, instead of being shown the living being of
a nation, we witness the dissection of a corpse. Pipes does
devote one chapter to the Church itself, which he sees only
as a civil institution and treats in the spirit of Soviet atheistic
propaganda. This people and this country are presented as
spiritually underdeveloped and motivated, from peasant to
tsar, exclusively by crude material interests. Even within the
sections devoted to individual topics there is no convincing,

[2] New York: Charles Scribner's Sons, 1974, 361 pp.

[3] Sergius of Radonezh (1314–1392), perhaps the best-loved Russian saint,
combined mystical spirituality with a practical concern for the Russian nation. In 1380 he gave his blessing to Dmitri, Prince of Moscow, to fight in a
battle that proved to be the first decisive Russian victory over the Mongol
occupiers.

St. Nil Sorsky (Nilus of Sora, 1433–1508) represents the mystical and
contemplative tradition of Eastern monasticism. He argued that the
Church and the State should be independent of each other. [Tr. note]

logical portrayal of history, but only a chaotic jumble of epochs and events from various centuries, often without so much as a date. The author willfully ignores those events, persons, or aspects of Russian life which would not prove conducive to his thesis, which is that the entire history of Russia has had but a single purpose—the creation of a police state. He selects only that which contributes to his derisive and openly hostile description of Russian history and the Russian people. The book allows only one possible conclusion to be drawn: that the Russian nation is anti-human in its essence, that it has been good for nothing throughout its thousand years of history, and that as far as any future is concerned, it is obviously a hopeless case. Pipes even bestows upon Emperor Nicholas I the distinction of having invented totalitarianism. Leaving aside the fact that it was not until Lenin that totalitarianism was ever actually implemented, Mr. Pipes, with all his erudition, should have been able to indicate that the idea of the totalitarian state was first proposed by Hobbes in his *Leviathan* (the head of the state is here said to have dominion not only over the citizens' lives and property, but also over their *conscience*). Rousseau, too, had leanings in this direction when he declared the democratic state to be "unlimited sovereign" not only over the possessions of its citizens, but over their *person* as well.

As a writer who has spent his whole life immersed in the Russian language and Russian folklore, I am particularly pained by one of Pipes's "scholarly" techniques. From among some forty thousand Russian proverbs, which in their unity and their inner contradictions make up a dazzling literary and philosophical edifice, Pipes wrests those half dozen (in Maxim Gorky's tendentious selection) that suit his needs, and uses them to "prove" the cruel and cynical nature of the Russian peasantry. This method affects me in much the same way as I imagine Rostropovich would feel if he had to listen to a wolf playing the cello.

There are two names that are repeated from book to book and article to article with a mindless persistence by all the scholars and essayists of this tendency: Ivan the Terrible and Peter the Great, to whom—implicitly or explicitly—they reduce the whole sense of Russian history. But one could just as easily find two or three kings no whit less cruel in the histories of England, France, or Spain, or indeed of any country, and yet no one thinks of reducing the complexity of historical meaning to such figures alone. And in any case, no two monarchs can determine the history of a thousand-year-old nation. But the refrain continues. Some scholars use this technique to show that communism is possible only in countries with a "morally defective" history, others in order to remove the stigma from communism itself, laying the blame for its incorrect implementation upon Russian national characteristics. Such a view was voiced in a number of recent articles devoted to the centenary of Stalin's birth, for instance in a piece by Professor Robert C. Tucker (*The New York Times*, 21 December 1979).

Tucker's short but vigorous article is astounding: surely this must have been written twenty-five years ago! How can a scholar and student of politics persist to this day in misunderstanding so fundamentally the phenomenon of communism? We are confronted yet again with those familiar, never-fading ideals of the revolution, which the despicable

Stalin ruined by ignoring Marx in favor of the abominable lessons of Russian history. Professor Tucker hastens to salvage socialism by suggesting that Stalin was not, after all, a *genuine* socialist! He did not act in accordance with Marxist theories, but trod in the footsteps of that wearisome pair, Ivan the Terrible from the sixteenth century and Peter the Great from the eighteenth. The whole Stalin era, we are to believe, is a *radical reversion* to the former tsarist era, and in no wise represents a consistent application of Marxism to contemporary realities; indeed, far from carrying on the Bolshevik cause, Stalin contributed to its destruction. Modesty prevents me from asking Professor Tucker to read at least the first volume of *The Gulag Archipelago*, and better still all three. But perhaps that would refresh his memory of how the communist police apparatus which would eventually grind up some sixty million victims was set up by Lenin, Trotsky, and Dzerzhinsky, first in the form of the Cheka, which had unlimited authority to execute unlimited numbers of people without trial; how Lenin drew up in his own hand the future Article 58 of the Criminal Code, on which the whole of Stalin's Gulag was founded;[4] and how the entire Red Terror and the repression of millions of peasants were formulated by Lenin and Trotsky. *These* instructions, at least, Stalin carried out conscientiously, albeit only to the extent of his limited intellectual abilities. The only respect in which he ventured to depart from Lenin was his destruction of the Communist Party leadership for the purpose of strengthening his own power. But even here he was merely

[4] On Lenin's contribution to the drafting of the Criminal Code, see *The Gulag Archipelago*, Vol. I, pp. 352–354. [Tr. note]

enacting a universal law of vast and bloody revolutions, which invariably devour their own creators. In the Soviet Union it used to be said with good reason that "Stalin is Lenin today," and indeed the entire Stalin period is a direct continuation of the Lenin era, only more mature in terms of its results and its long, uninterrupted development. No "Stalinism" has ever existed, either in theory or in practice; there was never any such phenomenon or any such era. This concept was invented after 1956 by intellectuals of the European Left as a way of salvaging the "ideals" of communism. And only by some evil figment of the imagination could Stalin be called a "Russian nationalist"—this of the man who exterminated fifteen million of the best Russian peasants, who broke the back of the Russian peasantry, and thereby of Russia herself, and who sacrificed the lives of more than thirty million people in the Second World War, which he waged without regard for less profligate means of warfare, without grudging the lives of the people.

Just what "model" could Stalin have seen in the former, tsarist Russia, as Tucker has it? Camps there were none; the very concept was unknown. Long-stay prisons were very few in number, and hence political prisoners—with the exception of terrorist extremists, but including all the Bolsheviks—were sent off to exile, where they were well fed and cared for at the expense of the state, where no one forced them to work, and whence any who so wished could flee abroad without difficulty. But even if we consider the number of nonpolitical prisoners at forced labor in those days, we find that it amounted to less than one ten-thousandth of the population of Gulag. All criminal investigations were conducted in strict compliance with established law, all trials were open and defendants were legally represented. The total number of secret police operatives in the whole country was less than that presently available to the KGB of the Ryazan district alone; secret police departments were located only in the three major cities and even there surveillance was weak, and anyone leaving the city limits immediately escaped observation. In the army there was no secret intelligence or surveillance whatsoever (a fact which greatly facilitated the February Revolution), since Nicholas II considered any activity of this type an insult to his army. To this we may add the absence of special border troops and fortified frontiers, and the complete freedom to emigrate.

In their presentation of prerevolutionary Russia, many Western historians succumb to a persistent but fallacious tradition, thereby to some extent echoing the arguments of Soviet propaganda. Before the outbreak of war in 1914, Russia could boast of a flourishing manufacturing industry, rapid growth, and a flexible, decentralized economy; its inhabitants were not constrained in their choice of economic activities, distinct progress was being made in the field of workers' legislation, and the material well-being of the peasants was at a level that has never been reached under the Soviet regime. Newspapers were free from preliminary political censorship (even during the war), there was complete cultural freedom, the intelligentsia was not restricted in its activity, religious and philosophical views of every shade were tolerated, and institutions of higher education enjoyed inviolable autonomy. Russia, with her many nationalities, knew no deportations of entire peoples and no armed separatist movements. This picture is not merely dissimilar to that of the communist era, but is in every respect its direct antithesis. Alexander I had even entered Paris with his army, but he did not annex an inch of European soil. Soviet conquerors never withdraw from any lands on which they once have set foot—and yet these are viewed as cognate phenomena! The "bad" Russia of old never loomed ominously over Europe, still less over America and Africa. She exported grain and butter, not arms and instructors in terrorism. And she collapsed out of loyalty to her Western allies, when Nicholas II prolonged the senseless war with Wilhelm instead of saving his country by concluding a separate peace (like Sadat today). Western animosity toward the former Russia was aroused by Russian revolutionaries in emigration, who propounded crude and simplistic views inspired by their political passions; these were never counterbalanced by responses or explanations from Russia, since no one there had any conception of the role of "agitation and propaganda." When, for example, on 9 January 1905, tragic events culminated in the death of about a hundred people during a St. Petersburg demonstration (no one was arrested), this came to be regarded as an inerasable stigma, a shameful episode which amply characterizes Russia. Yet the Soviet Union is not constantly reproached for the 17th of June 1953, when six hundred demonstrators in Berlin were killed in cold blood and fifty thousand more arrested. Indeed, such episodes seem to inspire respect for Soviet strength: "We must seek a common language."

Somehow, over the years, the friendship that existed between Russia and the young, newly formed United States in

16

the eighteenth century has been forgotten. Hostility toward Russia gained ground from the early twentieth century on. We are still witnessing its consequences today. But today these are much more than just remote sentiments; they threaten to lead the entire Western world into a fatal error.

4.

Misinformation by Informants

With American scholars demonstrating such a fundamental misunderstanding of Russia and the U.S.S.R., the blunders perpetrated by politicians come as less of a surprise. Although they are ostensibly men of action, their heads are ever under the sway of current theories and their hands shackled by the exigencies of the moment.

Only the combined effect of these factors can account for the notorious resolution on the "captive nations" (Public Law 86–90), passed by the U.S. Congress on 17 July 1959 and subsequently renewed: the manifest culprit, the U.S.S.R., is nowhere identified by name; world communism is referred to as "Russian"; Russia is charged with the subjugation of mainland China and Tibet and the Russians are denied a place on the roll of oppressed nations (which includes the nonexistent "Idel-Ural" and "Cossackia").

Ignorance and misunderstanding have clearly spread far beyond this one resolution.

Many present and former United States diplomats have also used their office and authority to help enshroud Soviet communism in a dangerous, explosive cloud of vaporous arguments and illusions. Much of this legacy stems from such diplomats of the Roosevelt school as Averell Harriman, who to this day assures gullible Americans that the Kremlin rulers are peace-loving men who just happen to be moved by heartfelt compassion for the wartime suffering of their Soviet people. (One need only recall the plight of the Crimean Tatars, who are still barred from returning to the Crimea for the sole reason that this would encroach upon Brezhnev's hunting estates.) In reality the Kremlin leadership is immeasurably indifferent to and remote from the Russian people, a people whom they have exploited to the point of total exhaustion and near extinction, and whom, when the need arises, they will mercilessly drive to destruction in their millions.

By means of his essays, public statements, and words of advice, all of which are supposedly rooted in a profound understanding of Soviet life, George Kennan has for years had a major detrimental influence upon the shape and direction of American foreign policy. He is one of the more persistent architects of the myth of the "moderates" in the Politburo, despite the fact that no such moderates have ever revealed themselves by so much as a hint. He is forever urging us to pay greater heed to the Soviet leaders' pronouncements and even today finds it inconceivable that anyone should mistrust Brezhnev's vigorous denials of aggressive intent. He prefers to ascribe the seizure of Afghanistan to the "defensive impulses" of the Soviet leadership. Many Western diplomats have abandoned painstaking analysis in favor of incurable self-delusion, as we can see in such a veteran of the political arena as Willy Brandt, whose *Ostpolitik* is suicidal for Germany. Yet these ruinous ventures are the very ones honored with Nobel Prizes for Peace.[5]

I would note here a tendency which might be called the "Kissinger syndrome," although it is by no means peculiar to him alone. Such individuals, while holding high office, pursue a policy of appeasement and capitulation, which sooner or later will cost the West many years and many lives, but immediately upon retirement the scales fall from their eyes and they begin to advocate firmness and resolution. How can this be? What caused the change? Enlightenment just doesn't come that suddenly! Might we not assume that they were well aware of the real state of affairs all along, but simply drifted with the political tide, clinging to their posts?

Long years of appeasement have invariably entailed the surrender of the West's positions and the bolstering of its adversary. Today we can assess on a global scale the achievement of the West's leading diplomats after thirty-five years of concerted effort: they have succeeded in strengthening the U.S.S.R. and Communist China in so many ways that only the ideological rift between those two regimes (for which the West can take no credit) still preserves the Western world from disaster. In other words, the survival of the West already depends on factors which are effectively beyond its control.

These diplomats still fall back on their precarious assumptions about an imaginary split within the Soviet Politburo

---

[5] The Nobel Peace Prize of 1971 was bestowed upon Willy Brandt, then the Chancellor of West Germany, for "concrete initiatives leading to the relaxation of tension" between East and West. [Tr. note]

between nonexistent "conservatives" and "liberals," "hawks" and "doves," "Right" and "Left," between old and young, bad and good—an exercise of surpassing futility. Never has the Politburo numbered a humane or peace-loving man among its members. The communist bureaucracy is not constituted to allow men of that caliber to rise to the top—they would instantly suffocate there.

Despite all this, America continues to be fed a soothing diet of fond hopes and illusions. Hopes have been expressed of a split in the Politburo, with one particular version claiming that it was not in fact Brezhnev who occupied Afghanistan! Or else leading experts have offered the fancy that "the U.S.S.R. will meet its Vietnam," be it in Angola, Ethiopia, or Afghanistan. (These experts and their readers may rest assured that the U.S.S.R. is at present quite capable of gobbling up five more such countries, swiftly and without choking.) And again and again we are asked to set our hopes on détente despite the trampling of yet another country. (There is indeed no cause for alarm here, for even after Afghanistan the Soviet leaders will be only too happy to restore détente to the *status quo ante*—an opportunity for them to purchase all that they require in between acts of aggression.)

It goes without saying that America will never understand the U.S.S.R. or fully grasp the danger it poses by relying on information from diplomats such as these.

But politicians of that ilk have lately been reinforced by recent émigrés from the Soviet Union, who have set about actively promoting their own spurious "explanation" of Russia and the U.S.S.R. There are no outstanding names among them, yet they earn prompt recognition as professors and

Russian specialists thanks to their sure sense of the kind of evidence that will find favor. They are persistent, outspoken, and repetitious contributors to the press of many countries, and the more or less concerted line which they take in their articles, interviews, and even books may be briefly summed up as follows: "collaboration with the communist government of the U.S.S.R., and war on Russian national consciousness." While these individuals were still in the U.S.S.R., they generally served the communist cause in various institutes, or were even actively employed for a number of years in the mendacious communist press, without ever voicing opposition. Then they emigrated from the Soviet Union on Israeli visas, without actually going to Israel (the Israelis term them "dropouts"). Having reached their destinations in the West, they immediately proclaimed themselves experts on Russia, on her history and national spirit, and on the life of the Russian people today—something they could not so much as observe from their privileged positions in Moscow. The most energetic of these new informants do not even blame the Soviet system for the sixty million lives it destroyed, or reproach it for its militant atheism. They condone its wholesale repression, while proclaiming Brezhnev a "peacemaker" and openly urging that the communist regime in the U.S.S.R. be given maximum support as the "lesser evil," the best alternative open to the West. Yet they simultaneously accuse the Russian national movement of this same kind of collaboration. The significance of the current spiritual processes in Russia is seriously misrepresented to the West. Western public opinion is being encouraged to respond with fear and even hatred to any revival in Russian national awareness, a sentiment that has been crushed almost to extinction by sixty years of communist power. In particular, contrived and disingenuous attempts have been made to link that revival with the government's calculated encouragement of anti-Semitism. For this purpose Soviet people are portrayed as nothing but a herd of sheep, utterly incapable of forming their own conclusions about their fate over the last sixty years or of understanding the cause of their poverty and suffering, entirely dependent upon official explanations from the communist leaders, and hence quite content to accept the anti-Semitic excuses which the government foists upon them. (In actual fact, the average Soviet citizen has a far shrewder understanding of the inhuman nature of communism than has many a Western essayist and politician.)

Several of these émigrés also indulge in rather uninformed digressions into earlier periods of Russian history, in close conformity with the above-mentioned myopic school of American historiography. Of the many members of this group we could here mention Dimitri Simes, or Alexander Yanov.[6] For seventeen years on end Yanov was a loyal communist journalist, who never spoke out against the regime, but now he glibly regales his credulous American readers

[6] Dimitri K. Simes was, until 1972, a staff member of the Institute of World Economy and International Relations in Moscow. He emigrated soon thereafter and is presently Director of Soviet Studies at Georgetown University's Center for Strategic and International Studies in Washington, D.C. He has written extensively on détente.

Alexander L. Yanov emigrated in 1974 and has been associated with the Institute of International Studies, University of California at Berkeley. He is the author of *Détente After Brezhnev* (1977) and *The Russian New Right* (1978). [Tr. note]

with distorted pictures of Soviet life or else skips lightly over the surface of Russian history, studiously avoiding its fundamental principles and blowing out one soap bubble after another. Simultaneously, and on almost consecutive pages, Yanov imputes to Russian national awareness two mutually exclusive tendencies: messianism (a bizarre fabrication), and isolationism, which for no apparent reason he regards as a threat to the rest of the world.

Given that a hostile and distorted portrayal of old Russia has been a tradition in American historical scholarship, seeds such as these are capable of bearing poisonous fruit.

The efforts of these tendentious informants have been supplemented and reinforced over the last year by a number of articles written by American journalists and in particular by the Moscow correspondents of American newspapers. The gist of these articles is more of the same: the grave threat which any rebirth of Russian national consciousness is said to pose to the West; an unabashed blurring of distinctions between Russian Orthodoxy and anti-Semitism (when it is not explicitly claimed that the two are identical, they are obtrusively juxtaposed in consecutive phrases and paragraphs); finally there is the extraordinary theory according to which the rising forces of national and religious consciousness and the declining, cynical communist leaders have but a single dream—to merge together into some sort of "New Right." The only puzzling question is what has been stopping them from doing just that for all these years? Who is there to forbid it? The truth of the matter is that religious and national circles in the U.S.S.R. have been systematically persecuted with the full force of the criminal code.

At first glance one is struck by how closely accounts by émigré informants and by free American correspondents co-incide: if two independent sources report one and the same thing, then there must surely be something to it. But one must take into account the circumstances under which all Western correspondents have to operate in the Soviet Union: authentic Soviet life, especially life in the provinces and in the rural districts, is hidden from their view by an impenetrable wall; any trips they make out of the city are purely cosmetic, and are carefully stage-managed by the KGB; moreover, it is extremely hazardous for ordinary Soviet people in the provinces to engage in conversation with a foreigner, other than at the KGB's behest. Typical is Robert Kaiser's admission that in the four years he spent as Moscow correspondent of the *Washington Post* he had heard no mention whatever of the massive Novocherkassk uprising of 1962![7] The Western correspondent relies for his information upon the following: a careful screening of the vacuous and sterile official Soviet press; off-the-record comments and speculations gleaned from Western diplomats (the sources coincide!); and chance encounters with middle-level representatives of the Soviet elite (but as human material this is too shoddy and unreliable to merit serious attention). Their chief source, however, is the conversations they have with those few Muscovites who have already irrevocably violated the ban on fraternizing with foreigners; usually these are representatives of the same Moscow circles to which the aforementioned émigré informants once belonged. They are

[7] On the Novocherkassk uprising, see *The Gulag Archipelago*, Vol. III, pp. 507–514. [Tr. note]

the chief source of information used in strident, doom-laden articles about the worldwide menace of Russian nationalism. And this is how some anonymous anti-Semitic leaflet in a Moscow gateway is taken up by the Western press and invested with universal significance. But it also explains why the sources so often agree: an image of the world is formed in accordance with its reflection in a single splinter of glass. In physics this is known as systematic instrument error.

But when some information happens to point in a different direction, when it fails to tally with what the Western press is presently looking for in Moscow, then it is simply suppressed. A case in point is the extremely important interview that Igor Shafarevich gave to Christopher Wren of *The New York Times*, but that was not published in the Western press. In the same way Western scholars and the Western press have been ignoring the *Herald of the Russian Christian Movement* [*Vestnik Russkogo Khristianskogo Dvizheniia*], a Paris-based journal which has been appearing for half a century; yet the journal enjoys great popularity in cultivated circles and is in fact published with their direct participation. Acquaintance with this journal would give Western commentators quite a different picture, far removed from the horrors they are wont to describe.

Only this absence of informed opinion can account for the warped view that the main problem in the U.S.S.R. today is that of emigration. How can the problems of any major country be reduced to the issue of who is allowed to depart from it? Here and there in the Russian provinces (Perm was a recent example) strikes involving many thousands of starving workers have been dispersed by force of arms (paratroops have even had to be dropped onto the factory roof)—but is the West alert enough to note all this and to react to it? And what of the far-reaching process that is now under way in Russia and is scheduled for completion in ten to fifteen years, a process threatening the very survival of the Russian people? It aims at nothing less than the final destruction of the Russian peasantry: huts and villages are being razed, peasants are being herded together in multi-storied settlements on the industrial model, links with the soil are being severed; national traditions, the national way of life, even apparently the Russian landscape and the national character—all are disappearing forever. And the reaction of the meager Western news media to this murderous communist onslaught on the very soul of our people? *They have not so much as noticed it!* In the first revolution (1917–1920), Lenin's curved dagger slashed at the throat of Russia. Yet Russia survived. In the second revolution (1929–1931) Stalin's sledgehammer strove to pound Russia to dust. Yet Russia survived. The third and final revolution is irrevocably under way, with Brezhnev's bulldozer bent on scraping Russia from the face of the earth. And at this moment, when Russian nationhood is being destroyed without pity, the Western media raise a hue and cry about the foremost threat to the world today—Russian national consciousness. . . .

5.

Russia Prostrate

Moscow is not the Soviet Union. Ever since the early 1930s, general living standards in the capital have been artificially boosted above the national level—by plundering the rest of the populace, particularly in rural areas. (The same is partially true of Leningrad and of certain restricted scientific settlements.) Thus for more than half a century the population of Moscow has had its diet artificially augmented and has been artificially maintained at a psychological level quite unlike that of the pillaged country at large. (The Bolsheviks learned the lesson of 1917, when the February Revolution broke out in hungry Petrograd.) As a result, Moscow has come to be a special little world, poised somewhere between the U.S.S.R. and the West: in terms of material comfort it is almost as superior to the rest of the Soviet Union as the West is superior to Moscow. However, this also means that any judgments based on Moscow experiences must be significantly corrected before they may be applied to Soviet experience in general. Authentic Soviet life is to be seen only in provincial towns, in rural areas, in the labor camps and in the harsh conditions of the peacetime army.

For my part, I spent the entire fifty-five years of my Soviet life in the remoter areas of the U.S.S.R., never enjoying the privileges of residence in the capital. I can thus draw upon my experiences without having to make any such correction, and my comments will consequently pertain not to Moscow, but to the country as a whole.

To begin with, the West's vision has been obscured by the false cliché according to which the Russians are the "ruling nationality" of the U.S.S.R. They are no such thing and never have been at any time since 1917. For the first fifteen years of Soviet power it fell to the Russians, Ukrainians, and Byelorussians to bear the crippling, devastating blow of communism (the declining birth rates of recent years have their roots in that period), and in the process their upper classes, clergy, cultural tradition, and intelligentsia, as well as the main food-producing section of the peasantry, were wiped out almost without trace. The finest names of the Russian past were outlawed and reviled, the country's history was systematically vilified, churches were obliterated in their tens of thousands, towns and streets were renamed in honor of executioners—a practice to be expected only of armies of occupation. But as the communists felt more firmly in control they dealt similar blows to each of the remaining national republics in turn, acting on a principle equally dear to Lenin, Hitler, and the common thug: always crush your enemies one by one. Thus in the U.S.S.R. there simply was no "ruling nationality": the communist internationalists never had need of one. The decision to retain Russian as the official language was purely mechanical; one language after all had to serve in this capacity. The sole effect of this use of Russian has been to defile the language; it has not encouraged Russians to think of themselves as masters: just because a rapist addresses his victim in her own language, this does not make it any less of a rape. And the fact that from the end of the 1930s the communist leadership came to be increasingly composed of men of Russian and Ukrainian origin did absolutely nothing to raise those nations to hegemony. The same law operates throughout the world (in China too, and in Korea): to cast in one's lot with the communist leadership is to repudiate not only one's own nation but humankind itself.

But the bigger sheep yields more fleece, and so throughout the Soviet period it has been the R.S.F.S.R.[8] which has borne the main brunt of economic oppression. Fearing an outbreak of national resistance, the authorities were a little more cautious in applying economic measures to the other national republics. The inhuman kolkhoz system was installed everywhere; nevertheless, the profit margin on a hundredweight of oranges in Georgia was incomparably more favorable than that on a hundredweight of Russian potatoes harvested with greater expenditure of labor. Each of the republics was exploited without mercy, but the ultimate degree of exploitation was reached in the R.S.F.S.R., and today the most poverty-stricken rural areas of the U.S.S.R. are the Russian villages. The same is true of Russian provincial towns, which have not seen meat, butter, or eggs for decades

[8] R.S.F.S.R. is the official designation of that portion of the country which remains when the fourteen outlying "national republics" are excluded.

and which can only dream of even such simple fare as macaroni and margarine.

Subsistence at such an abysmally low level—for half a century!—is leading to a biological degeneration of the people, to a decline in its physical and spiritual powers, a process that is intensified by mind-numbing political propaganda, by the violent eradication of religion, by the suppression of every sign of culture, by a situation where drunkenness is the only form of freedom, where women are doubly exhausted (by working for the state on an equal footing with men and also in the home, without the aid of domestic appliances), and where the minds of its children are systematically deprived. Public morality has declined drastically, not due to any inherent failing in the people, but because the communists have denied it sustenance, both physical and spiritual, and have disposed of all those who could provide spiritual relief, above all the priesthood.

Russian national consciousness today has been suppressed and humiliated to an extraordinary degree by all that it has endured and continues to endure. It is the consciousness of a man whose long illness has brought him to the point of death and who can dream only of rest and recuperation. The thoughts and aspirations of a family in the depths of Russia are immeasurably more modest and timid than the Western correspondent can possibly gather from his leisurely Moscow chats. This is how their thoughts run: if only the petty local communist despot would somehow quit his uncontrolled tyranny; if only they could get enough to eat for once, and buy shoes for the children, and lay in enough fuel for the winter;

if only they could have sufficient space to live even two to a room; if only a church would be opened within a hundred miles of where they live; if only they weren't forbidden to baptize their children and bring them up knowing right from wrong; and if only they could get Father away from the bottle.

And it is *this* yearning on the part of the Russian hinterland to rise and live like men, not beasts, to regain some portion of its religious and national consciousness, which the West's glib and garrulous informants today label "Russian chauvinism" and the supreme threat to contemporary mankind, a menace greater by far than the well-fed dragon of communism whose paw is already raised, bristling with tanks and rockets, over what remains of our planet. It is *these* unfortunates, this mortally ill people, helpless to save itself from ruin, who are credited with fanatical messianism and militant nationalism!

This is just a phantom to scare the gullible. The simple love of one's mother country, an inborn feeling of patriotism, is today branded "Russian nationalism." But no one can possibly incite to militant nationalism a country that for fifty years has not even had enough bread to eat. It is not the average Russian who feels compelled to hold other nations captive, to keep Eastern Europe encaged, to seize and arm far-off lands; this answers only the malignant needs of the Politburo. As for "historical Russian messianism," this is contrived nonsense: it has been several centuries since any section of the government or intelligentsia influential in the spiritual life of the country has suffered from the disease of messianism. Indeed, it seems inconceivable to me that in our sordid age any people on earth would have the gall to deem itself "chosen."

All the peoples of the Soviet Union need a long period of convalescence after the ravages of communism, and for the Russian people, which endured the most violent and protracted onslaught of all, it will take perhaps 150 or 200 years of peace and national integrity to effect a recovery. But a Russia of peace and national integrity is inimical to the communist madness. A Russian national reawakening and liberation would mark the downfall of Soviet and with it of world communism. And Soviet communism is well aware that it is being abrogated by the Russian national consciousness. For those who genuinely love Russia no reconciliation with communism has ever been possible or ever will be. That is why communism has always been most ruthless of all in its treatment of Christians and advocates of national rebirth. In the early years this meant wholesale execution; later the victims were left to rot in the camps. But to this very day the persecution continues inexorably: Vladimir Shelkov was done to death by twenty-five years in the camps,[9] Ogurtsov has already served thirteen years and Osipov twelve;[10] this winter the completely apolitical "Christian Committee for the Defense of Believers' Rights in the

[9] Vladimir Shelkov, head of the independent branch of the Adventist Church in the Soviet Union, died in a strict-regime camp in January 1980. He was eighty-four years old. [Tr. note]

[10] Igor Ogurtsov headed an organization that advocated the rebuilding of Russia on Christian principles. Arrested in 1967, he was sentenced to twenty years of imprisonment and exile.

Vladimir Osipov, editor of *Veche*, a Samizdat journal dedicated to religious and nationalist themes, was sentenced to eight years in 1975. He had also served an earlier term for dissident activities. [Tr. note]

34

U.S.S.R." was smashed;[11] the independent priests Father Gleb Yakunin and Father Dimitri Dudko have been arrested,[12] and the members of Ogorodnikov's Christian seminar have been hauled off to prison.[13] The authorities make no attempt to hide the fact that they are crushing the Christian faith with the full force of their machinery of terror. And at this moment, when religious circles in the U.S.S.R. are being persecuted with such unmitigated ferocity—how fine and edifying it is to hear Russian Orthodoxy reviled by the Western press!

The present anti-Russian campaign by those who provide the West with its information is beginning to flourish even in the foremost American newspapers and journals and it is of the greatest value and comfort to Soviet communism (although I do not wish to insist that the whole campaign is necessarily Soviet-inspired).

For the West, on the other hand, this campaign stands the facts on their head, inducing it to fear its natural ally—the oppressed Russian people—and to trust its mortal foe, the communist regime. The West is persuaded to send this regime lavish aid, which it so badly needs after half a century of economic bankruptcy.

[11] The "Christian Committee" was formed in 1976. [Tr. note]

[12] Fr. Gleb Yakunin, a founding member of the "Christian Committee" and an outspoken critic of the compliant policies of the Moscow Patriarchate, was arrested in November 1979.

Fr. Dimitri Dudko brought hundreds of persons, including many students and intellectuals, into the Russian Orthodox Church, largely through his remarkable sermons. He was arrested in January 1980. [Tr. note]

[13] In 1974 Aleksandr Ogorodnikov launched a study group in Moscow for the discussion of religious and philosophical issues. The idea caught on in university circles and soon similar Christian seminars were organized in Leningrad, Smolensk, and other cities. Ogorodnikov was arrested in 1978, several other leading figures in 1979. [Tr. note]

6.

When Is Communism in the Saddle?

But even a humbled, defeated, and despoiled nation continues to exist physically, and the aim of the communist authorities (whether in the U.S.S.R., in China, or in Cuba) is to force the people to serve them unfailingly as a work force or, if need be, as a fighting force. However, when it comes to war, communist ideology has long since lost all its drawing power in the U.S.S.R.; it inspires no one. The regime's intention is thus obvious: to take that same Russian national sentiment which they themselves have been persecuting and to exploit it once more for their new war, for their brutal imperialistic ambitions; indeed, to do so with ever greater frenzy and desperation as communism grows ideologically moribund, in a bid to derive from national sentiments the strength and fortitude they lack. This is certainly a real danger.

The informants discussed earlier see this danger, indeed they recognize nothing *but* this danger (rather than the true aspirations of the national spirit). Hence, at their bluntest they abuse us in advance as chauvinists and fascists, while at their most circumspect they argue as follows: Since you can see that any religious and national renascence of the Russian people may be exploited by the Soviet authorities for their own vile purposes, you must renounce not only this renascence but any national aspirations whatever.

But then the Soviet authorities also try to exploit the Jewish emigration from the U.S.S.R. in order to fan the flames of anti-Semitism, and not without success ("See that? They're the only ones allowed to escape from this hell, and the West sends goods to pay for it!"). Does it follow that we are entitled to advise Jews to forgo the quest for their spiritual and national origins? Of course not. Are we not all entitled to live our natural life on the earth and to strive toward our individual goals, without heed for what others may think or what the papers may write, and without worrying about the dark forces that may attempt to exploit those goals for their own ends?

And why should we speak only about the future? We have our recent past to draw on. In 1918–1922 throughout Russia, throngs of peasants with pitchforks (and even in some recorded cases bearing only icons) marched in their thousands against the machine guns of the Red Army; in Bolshevism they saw a force inimical to their very existence as a nation. And in their thousands they were slaughtered.

And what of 1941–1945? It was then that communism first succeeded in saddling and bridling Russian nationalism: millions of lives were affected and it took place in full view of the rest of the world; the murderer saddled his half-dead victim, but in America or Britain no one was appalled; the whole Western world responded with unanimous enthusiasm, and "Russia" was forgiven for all the unpleasant associations her name aroused and for all past sins and omissions. For the first time she became the object of infatuation and applause (paradoxically, even as she ceased being herself), because this saddle horse was then saving the Western world from Hitler. Nor did we hear any reproaches about this being the "supreme danger," although that is in fact precisely what it was. At the time, the West refused even to entertain the thought that the Russians might have any feelings other than communist ones.

But what were the real feelings of the peoples under Soviet dominion? Here is how it was. June 22, 1941, had just reverberated into history, Old Man Stalin had sobbed out his bewildered speech,[14] and the entire working population of adult age and of whatever nationality (not the younger generation, cretinized by Marxism) held its breath in anticipation: Our bloodsuckers have had it! We'll soon be free now. This damned communism is done for! Lithuania, Latvia, and Estonia gave the Germans a jubilant welcome. Byelorussia, the Western Ukraine, and the first occupied Russian territories followed suit. But the mood of the people was demonstrated most graphically of all by the Red Army: before the eyes of the whole world it retreated along a 2,000-kilometer front, on foot, but every bit as fast as motorized units. Nothing could possibly be more convincing than the way

[14] On July 3, 1941, almost two weeks after Germany's attack on the U.S.S.R., Stalin made his first wartime radio address to the nation. In a voice heavy with emotion, he addressed his listeners as "brothers and sisters" and "friends." [Tr. note]

these men, soldiers in their prime, voted with their feet. Numerical superiority was entirely with the Red Army, they had excellent artillery and a strong tank force, yet back they rolled, a rout without compare, unprecedented in the annals of Russian and world history. In the first few months some three million officers and men had fallen into enemy hands!

That is what the popular mood was like—the mood of peoples some of whom had lived through twenty-four years of communism and others but a single year.[15] For them the whole point of this latest war was to cast off the scourge of communism. Naturally enough, each people was primarily bent not on resolving any European problem but on its own national task—liberation from communism.

Did the West see this catastrophic retreat? It could not do otherwise. But did it learn any lessons from it? No, blinded by its own pains and anxieties, it has failed to grasp the point to this very day. Yet if it had been unflinchingly committed to the principle of *universal* liberty, it should not have used Lend-Lease to buy the murderous Stalin's help, and should not have strengthened his dominion over nations which were seeking their own freedom. The West should have opened an independent front against Hitler and crushed him by *its own* efforts. The democratic countries had the strength to achieve this, but they grudged it, preferring to shield themselves with the unfortunate peoples of the U.S.S.R.

After twenty-four years of terror, no amount of persuasion could have enabled communism to save its skin by sad-

[15] A number of countries and territories were annexed by the U.S.S.R. in 1939–1940. These included Western Ukraine and Western Byelorussia (detached from Poland in 1939), Estonia, Latvia, Lithuania, Northern Bukovina, and Bessarabia. [Tr. note]

dling Russian nationalism. But as it turned out (deprived of outside information in the hermetically sealed communist world, we had no way of anticipating this), another, similar scourge was bearing down on us from the West, one, moreover, with its own special anti-national mission: to annihilate the Russian people in part and to enslave the survivors. And the first thing the Germans did was to restore the collective farms (whose members had scattered in all directions) in order to exploit the peasantry more efficiently. Thus the Russian people were caught between hammer and anvil; faced with two ferocious adversaries, they were bound to favor the one who spoke their own language. Thus was our nationalism forced to don the saddle and bridle of communism. At a stroke, communism seemed to forget its own slogans and doctrines, remaining deaf to them for several years to come; it forgot Marxism, whereas phrases about "glorious Russia" never left its lips; it even went so far as to restore the Church—but all this lasted only until the end of the war. And so our victory in this ill-starred war served only to tighten the yoke about our necks.

But there was also a Russian movement which sought a third path: attempting to take advantage of this war and in spite of the odds to liberate Russia from communism. Such men were in no sense supporters of Hitler; their integration into his empire was involuntary and in their hearts they regarded only the Western countries as their allies (moreover, they felt this sincerely, with none of the duplicity of the communists). For the West, however, anyone who wanted to liberate himself from communism in that war was regarded as a traitor to the cause of the West. Every nation in the

U.S.S.R. could be wiped out for all the West cared, and any number of millions could die in Soviet concentration camps, just as long as it could get out of this war successfully and as quickly as possible. And so hundreds of thousands of these Russians and Cossacks, Tatars and Caucasian nationals were sacrificed; they were not even allowed to surrender to the Americans, but were turned over to the Soviet Union, there to face reprisals and execution.

Even more shocking is the way the British and American armies surrendered into the vengeful hands of the communists hundreds of thousands of peaceful civilians, convoys of old men, women, and children, as well as ordinary Soviet POWs and forced laborers used by the Germans—surrendered them against their will, and even after witnessing the suicide of some of them. And British units shot, bayoneted, and clubbed these people who for some reason did not wish to return to their homeland. More amazing still is the fact that not only were none of these British and American officers ever punished or reprimanded, but for almost thirty years the free, proud, and unfettered press of these two countries unanimously and with studied innocence kept its silence about their governments' act of treachery. For thirty years not a single honest pen presented itself! Surely this is the most astonishing fact of all! In this single instance the West's unbroken tradition of publicity suddenly failed. Why?

At the time, it seemed more advantageous to buy off the communists with a couple of million foolish people and in this way to purchase perpetual peace.

42

In the same way—and without any real need—the whole of Eastern Europe was sacrificed to Stalin.

Now, thirty-five years later, we can sum up the cost of this wisdom: the security of the West today is solely dependent upon the unforeseen Sino-Soviet rift.

7.

A Succession of Errors

The selfish and ruinous mistake that the West committed during World War II has since been repeated time and time again, always in the fervent hope of avoiding a confrontation with communism. The West has done its utmost to ignore communist mass murder and aggression. It promptly forgave East Berlin (1953) as well as Budapest and Prague. It hastened to believe in the peaceful intentions of North Korea (which will yet show its true worth) and in the nobility of North Vietnam. It has allowed itself to be shamefully duped over the Helsinki agreement (for which it paid by recognizing forever all the communist takeovers in Europe). It seized on the myth of a progressive Cuba (even Angola, Ethiopia, and South Yemen have not sufficed to disenchant Senator McGovern), and put its faith in the alleged key to salvation represented by Eurocommunism. It solemnly participated in the interminable sessions of the sham Vienna Conference on European Disarmament. And after April 1978, it tried for almost two years not to notice the seizure of Afghanistan. Historians and future observers will be amazed and at a loss to explain such cowardly blindness. Only the appalling Cambodian genocide has exposed to the West the depth of the lethal abyss (familiar to us, who have lived there for sixty years), but even here, it seems, the Western conscience is already becoming inured and distracted.

It is high time for all starry-eyed dreamers to realize that the nature of communism is one and the same the whole world over, that it is everywhere inimical to the national welfare, invariably striving to destroy the national organism in which it is developing, before moving on to destroy adjacent organisms. No matter what the illusions of détente, no one will ever achieve a stable peace with communism, which is capable only of voracious expansion. Whatever the latest act in the charade of détente, communism continues to wage an incessant ideological war in which the West is unfailingly referred to as the enemy. Communism will never desist from its efforts to seize the world, be it through direct military conquest, through subversion and terrorism, or by subtly undermining society from within. Italy and France are still free, but they have already allowed themselves to be corroded by powerful communist parties. Every human being and any society (especially a democracy) tries to hope for the best; this is only natural. But in the case of communism, there is simply nothing to hope for: no reconciliation with communist doctrine is possible. The alternatives are either its complete triumph throughout the world or else its total collapse everywhere. The only salvation for Russia, for China, and for the entire world lies in a renunciation of this doctrine. Otherwise the world will face inexorable ruin. The communist occupation of Eastern Europe and East Asia will not come to an end; indeed there is an imminent danger of a takeover in Western Europe and many other parts of the world. The prospects for communism in Latin America and Africa have already been clearly demonstrated; in fact, any country that is not careful can be seized. There is of course the hope that things will turn out differently: that the communist aggressors will ultimately fail, like all aggressors in the past. They themselves believe that their hour of world conquest has arrived, and scenting victory, they unwittingly hasten—to their doom. But to achieve such an outcome in a future war would cost mankind billions of casualties.

In view of this mortal danger, one might have thought that American diplomatic efforts would be directed above all toward reducing the threatening might of these imperialistic "horsemen," to ensuring that they will never again succeed in bridling the national feelings of any country and drawing upon the vitality of its people. Yet this path has not been followed; in fact, the opposite course of action has been pursued.

American diplomacy over the last thirty-five years presents a spectacle of sorry bumbling. The United States, only recently the dominant world power, the victor in World War II and the leader in the United Nations, has seen a steady, rapid, and often humiliating erosion of its position at the U.N. and in the world at large, a process even its Western European allies have come to condone. It has continually declined vis-à-vis the U.S.S.R.: things have reached the point where American senators make apologetic visits to Moscow in order to ensure that the debates in the Senate are not taken amiss in the Kremlin. The whole thrust of American diplomacy has been directed to postponing any conflict, even at the cost of progressively diminishing American strength.

The lesson of World War II is that only desperate, pitiless circumstances can bring about any cooperation between communism and the nation it has enslaved. The United States has not learned this lesson: the Soviet and Eastern European governments have been treated as the genuine spokesmen of the national aspirations of the peoples they have subjugated, and the false representatives of these regimes have been dealt with respectfully. This amounts to a rejection—in advance, and in a form most detrimental to American interests—of any future alliance with the oppressed peoples, who are thereby driven firmly into the clutches of communism. This policy leaves the Russian and the Chinese people in bitter and desperate isolation—something the Russians already tasted in 1941.

In the 1950s, an eminent representative of the postwar Russian emigration submitted to the U.S. Administration a project for coordinating the efforts of Russian anti-communist forces. The response was formulated by a high-ranking American official: "We have no need of any kind of Russia, whether future or past." A conceited, mindless, and suicidal answer as far as American interests are concerned. The world has now come to the point where without the rebirth of a healthy, national-minded Russia, America itself will not survive, since all would be annihilated in the bloody clash. In that struggle it would be ruinous for America to fail to distinguish, in theory and in practice, between the communist aggressors and the peoples of the U.S.S.R. so tragically drawn into the conflict. It would be disastrous to fight "the Russians" instead of communism and thereby force a repetition of 1941, when the Russians will again grasp at freedom and find no helping hand.

The day-to-day implementation of current American foreign policy has served to support this perverse and pernicious surrender of the Russian national consciousness to its communist taskmaster. And now, after thirty-five years of failure, American diplomacy has gambled on another short-sighted, unwise—indeed mad—policy: to use China as a shield, which means in effect abandoning the national forces of China as well, and driving them completely under the communist yoke. (In the interests of this policy it was even deemed acceptable to contribute Taiwan as a down payment.)

This act of betrayal is a blow to the national feelings of both Chinese *and* Russians. ("America is openly supporting our totalitarian oppressors and equipping them against us!")

I hardly dare ask where that leaves the principles of democracy. Where is the vaunted respect for the freedom of all nations? But even in purely strategic terms this is a short-sighted policy: a fateful reconciliation of the two communist regimes could occur overnight, at which point they could unite in turning against the West. But even without such a reconciliation, a China armed by America would be more than a match for America.

The strategic error of not realizing that the oppressed peoples are allies of the West has led Western governments to commit a number of irreparable blunders. For many years they could have had free access to the oppressed people via the airwaves. But this means was either not used at all or else used incompetently. It would have been an easy matter for America to relay television broadcasts to the Soviet Union via satellite, but it was easier still to abandon this project after angry protests from the Soviet regime (which knows what to fear). It goes without saying that this medium would require a proper appreciation for the needs and intellectual concerns of the suffering people to whom it is addressed. And it also goes without saying that offensive commercial broadcasts are not what is needed—this would merely be an affront to the hungry viewers, and would be worse than nothing.

The defective information about the U.S.S.R. that reaches America brings about a mutual lack of communication, and as a result Americans, too, find it difficult to understand what they look like from the other side. A case in point is the Russian section of the Voice of America, which seems to go out of its way to repel the thoughtful Russian listener from any understanding of America, to alienate his sympathies, and even to shock and distress him.

The West is incapable of creating balanced and effective broadcasts to the Soviet Union precisely because information about the U.S.S.R. is received in the West in skewed and distorted form. The Russian section of the Voice of America, with its large staff and considerable budget, serves American interests poorly, in fact frequently does them great disservice. Apart from news and topical political commentary, hours of the daily program are filled with trite and inconsequential drivel which can do nothing but irritate the hungry and oppressed millions of listeners whose paramount need is to be told the truth about their own history. Instead of transmitting this history to them (with frequent repetition to compensate for the difficulties of radio reception), together with readings from those books the very possession of which is punishable by imprisonment in the U.S.S.R., instead of bolstering the anti-communist spirit of these potential allies of the U.S.A., hours of radio time are filled with frivolous reports on enthusiastic collectors of beer bottles and on the delights of ocean cruises (the fine food, the casino and discotheque are described with particular relish), with biographical details about American pop singers, any amount of sports news, which the citizens of the U.S.S.R. are not prevented from knowing anyway, and jazz, which they can pick up without difficulty from any of the other foreign stations. (Hardly more felicitous is the policy of broadcasting accounts by recent Jewish immigrants to the U.S.A., who tell in great detail about their life, their new jobs, and about how happy they are here. Since it is common knowledge in the U.S.S.R. that only Jews have the right to emigrate, these programs serve no purpose except to further the growth of anti-Semitism.) It is clear that the directors of the Voice of America are constantly trying not to arouse the anger of the Soviet leadership. In their zeal to serve détente, they remove from their programs everything that might irritate the communists in power. There are plenty of examples of such political kowtowing to the Central Committee of the CPSU, but I will cite two instances from my own experience, simply because they are easier for me to document. My statement concerning the arrest of Alexander Ginzburg on 4 February 1977 consisted of only three sentences, of which the following two were cut by the censors at VOA:

> This reprisal affects people in the West far more than it might seem at first sight. It is a significant step in the unremitting and all-inclusive policy of securing the Soviet rear in order to facilitate the offensive operation which it has been conducting so successfully over the last few years and which can only be intensified in the future: an assault on the strength, spirit, and the very existence of the West.

My statement to the 1977 Sakharov Hearings in Rome was completely rejected by VOA because of the following passage:

> ... [I would like] to hope that the spine-chilling accounts heard from your rostrum might pierce the deafness of material well-being which will respond only to the trumpet of doom but heeds no lesser sound. May they penetrate the awareness of those short-sighted individuals who are content to relax and to bask in the venomous melodies of Eurocommunism.

The chaste guardians of the VOA could not permit such words to reach the ears of its listeners in the East, or, for that matter, in the West. But this is not the worst of it: at times the Voice of America dances to the tune called by the communist regime or indeed becomes indistinguishable from a Moscow radio station. A recent broadcast apropos of Tito's illness announced that there was also "joyful news" to report from Yugoslavia: in the days of their leader's illness, thousands of citizens are eagerly joining the Party! Is this really any different from the insulting Leninist-Stalinist drivel that blares forth every day from Soviet loudspeakers? Such a broadcast can only cause Soviet listeners to doubt the mental competence of those who transmit it. And the religious program almost completely excludes Orthodox services, which are what Russian listeners most need, deprived as they are of churches. In the meager time slot available to religion as a whole, Orthodoxy is curtailed (as it is curtailed in the U.S.S.R.) because it is "a religion uncharacteristic of the U.S.A." This may be so, but it is surely characteristic of Russia! And the broadcast *is* conducted in Russian.

If we add to this the fact that the broadcasts are presented in a language difficult to acknowledge as Russian (replete with crude grammatical errors, poor syntax, inadequate enunciation, and misplaced stress), then it is fair to conclude that every reasonable effort has been made to turn away Russian listeners from this radio station.

This is an inept utilization of the mightiest weapon that the United States possesses to create mutual understanding (or even an alliance) between America and the oppressed Russian people.

It is true that other Western Russian-language radio stations have similar defects. The BBC, too, shows a marked eagerness not to offend communist sensibilities and a superficial understanding of the Russian people of today; this leads to an inability to select what is genuinely important for its listeners, and many valuable hours of broadcasting time are taken up with worthless and irrelevant twaddle.

8.

What My *Letter to the Soviet Leaders* Attempted to Do

For the multinational human mass confined today within the boundaries of the Soviet Union, there are only two possibilities: either a brutally imperialistic development of communism, with the subjugation of countries in many parts of the globe, or else a renunciation of communist ideology and a shift to a path of reconciliation, recovery, love of one's country, and care for one's people.

As a Russian, I find little consolation in the thought that Soviet communism might after all suffer defeat in the pursuit of the first alternative, and that a certain number of today's bosses (those who fail to make a getaway) will face a military tribunal on the Nuremberg model. There is no comfort in this thought because the human cost of achieving this outcome would fall most heavily on the deceived and afflicted Russian people.

But how to make the second alternative attainable? It is extraordinarily difficult to achieve such an outcome with indigenous strength alone in the conditions of a communist dictatorship, especially because the rest of the world, in its blindness, shows little sympathy for our attempts to free ourselves from communism, and at best washes its hands of us.

When I came to understand this problem, I decided seven years ago to undertake an action which it was within my limited powers to accomplish: I wrote my *Letter to the Soviet Leaders*, in which I call on them to shake off the communist delirium and to minister to their own devastated country.[16] The chances of success were naturally almost nil, but my aim was at least to pose the question loudly and publicly. If not the current leaders, then perhaps one of their successors might take note of my proposals. In the *Letter* I attempted to formulate the minimum national policy that could be implemented without wresting power from the incumbent communist rulers. (It would surely have been entirely unrealistic to expect them to relinquish their personal power.) I proposed that they should discard communist ideology, at least for the time being. (But how painful it would be to renounce this weapon, insomuch as it is precisely to communist ideas that the West yields most readily! . . .)

In the sphere of foreign policy, my proposal foresaw the following consequences: We were not to "concern ourselves with the fortunes of other hemispheres," we were to "renounce unattainable and irrelevant missions of world domination," to "give up our Mediterranean aspirations," and to "abandon the financing of South American revolutionaries." Africa should be left in peace; Soviet troops should be with-

[16] The *Letter* was sent to its addressees in September 1973. The Russian text and its English translation were published in 1974. [Tr. note]

drawn from Eastern Europe (so that these puppet regimes would be left to face their own people without the support of Soviet divisions); no peripheral nation should be forcibly kept within the bounds of our country; the youth of Russia should be liberated from universal, compulsory military service. As I wrote: "The demands of internal growth are incomparably more important to us, as a people, than the need for any external expansion of our power."

The reaction of the addressees to my proposal was hardly surprising: they didn't bat an eye. But the reaction of the Western and in particular the American press simply astonished me. My program was construed as conservative, retrograde, isolationist, and as a tremendous threat to the world! It would seem that the consciousness of the West has been so debilitated by decades of capitulation that when the Soviet Union, after seizing half of Europe, ventures into Asia and Africa, this evokes respect: we must not anger them, we must try to find a common language with these progressive forces (no doubt a confusion with "aggressive" here). Yet when I called for an immediate halt to all aggression, and to any thought of aggression, when I proposed that all those peoples who so wished should be free to secede, and that the Soviet Union should look to its domestic problems, this was interpreted as and even noisily proclaimed to be reactionary and dangerous isolationism.

But at the very least, one should be able to draw a distinction between the isolationism of the world's chief defender (the United States) and the isolationism of the world's major assailant (the Soviet Union). The former withdrawal is certainly a grave danger to the world and to peace in general, while the latter would be highly beneficial. If Soviet (and to-day also Cuban and Vietnamese, tomorrow Chinese) troops would cease taking over the world and would go home, whom would this endanger? Could someone explain this to me? I cannot understand to this day.

Furthermore, I never proposed any kind of total isolationism (involving cultural and economic withdrawal, for instance), nor did I call for Russia to sequester herself as if there were no one else on the globe. To my nation—an organism gravely ill after sixty years of communism and after sixty million human victims (not counting war casualties)—I offered the only advice that can be offered to someone so seriously afflicted: Stop wasting your valuable strength on fighting and pushing around healthy people; concentrate on your own recovery, conserving to this end every grain of the nation's strength. "Let us find strength, sense and courage to put our own house in order before we busy ourselves with the cares of the entire planet"; "the physical and spiritual health of the people must be the goal." I envisaged an ascent from the material and moral abyss in which the people find themselves today. Children were to be preserved from having their heads stuffed with ideology, women were to be shielded from backbreaking physical labor, men saved from alcohol, and nature protected from poison; the shattered family upbringing was to be restored; schools were to be improved and the Russian language itself saved before it could be destroyed by the communist system. To achieve all this would require some 150 to 200 years of external peace and patient concentration on internal problems. Whom could this possibly endanger?

But this letter was a genuine address to very real rulers

possessed of immeasurable power, and it was plain that the very most one could hope for would be concessions on their side, certainly not capitulation: neither free general elections nor a complete (or even partial) change of leadership could be expected. The most I called for was a renunciation of communist ideology and of its most cruel consequences, so as to allow at least a little more breathing space for the national spirit, for throughout history only national-minded individuals have been able to make constructive contributions to society. And the only path down from the icy cliff of totalitariansim that I could propose was the slow and smooth descent via an authoritarian system. (If an unprepared people were to jump off that cliff directly into democracy, it would be crushed to an anarchical pulp.) This "authoritarianism" of mine also drew immediate fire in the Western press.

But in the *Letter* I qualified this concept then and there: "an authoritarian order founded on love of one's fellow man"; "an authoritarianism with a firm basis in laws that reflect the will of the people"; "a calm and stable system" which does not "degenerate into arbitrariness and tyranny"; a renunciation, "once and for all, of psychiatric violence and secret trials, and of that brutal, immoral trap which the camps represent"; the toleration of all religions; "free art and literature, the untrammeled publication of books." I doubt that anyone can offer any temporary measures more beneficial than these to take effect after we emerge from our prison.

As concerns the theoretical question whether Russia should choose or reject authoritarianism in the future, I have no final opinion, and have not offered any. My criticism of certain aspects of democracy is well known. I do not think

59

that the will of the English people was implemented when England was for years sapped of its strength by a Labor government—elected by only forty percent of the voters. Nor was the will of the German people served when the Left bloc had a majority of one seat in the Bundestag. Nor is any nation served when half the electorate is so disillusioned that it stays away from the polling booths. I cannot count among the virtues of democracy its impotence vis-à-vis small groups of terrorists, its inability to prevent the growth of organized crime, or to check unrestrained profiteering at the expense of public morality. And I would note that the terrifying phenomenon of totalitarianism, which has been born into our world perhaps four times, did not issue from authoritarian systems, but in each case from a weak democracy: the one created by the February Revolution in Russia, the Weimar and the Italian republics, and Chiang Kai-shek's China. The majority of governments in human history have been authoritarian, but they have yet to give birth to a totalitarian regime.

I have never attempted to analyze this whole question in theoretical terms, nor do I intend to do so now, for I am neither a political scientist nor a politician. I am simply an artist who is distressed by the painfully clear events and crises of today. And in any case the problem cannot, I think, be settled by any journalistic debate or any hasty advice, even if it be buttressed by scholarship. The answer can only emerge through an organic development of accumulated national experience, and it must be free of any external coercion.

Here I would like to point once more to the respectful consideration which scholarship has always accorded the various unique features in the cultural development of even the smallest nations of Africa or Asia. And I would simply ask that the Russian people not be denied the same kind of treatment and that we not be dictated to, just as Africa is not. The Russian people have a 1,100-year-long history— longer than that of many of Russia's impatient teachers. Over this long period the Russians have created a large store of their own traditional social concepts, which outside observers should not dismiss with a sneer. Here are a few examples. The traditional medieval Russian concept of justice (*pravda*)[17] was understood as justice in the ultimate sense. It was an ontological rather than a juridical concept, something granted by God. The social ideal was to live justly (*pravedno*), that is, live on a higher moral plane than any possible legal requirement. (This of course does not mean that everyone lived up to such precepts, but the ideal was accepted by all.) A number of Russian proverbs reflect this concern:

The world itself weighs less than one just word (*odno slovo pravdy*).

The Lord resides in justice (*v pravde*), not in strength.

If all men lived justly (*po pravde*), no laws would be needed.

According to another traditional Russian concept, the truth cannot be determined by voting, since the majority does not necessarily have any deeper insight into the truth. (And

[17] In modern Russian, this word means "truth." In medieval Russia, this term signified "justice," "right," as well as "law" in the broad sense. The first Russian code of laws (eleventh century) was called *Pravda Russkaya*. [Tr. note]

what we know of mass psychology would suggest that the reverse is often true.) When representatives of the entire country gathered for important decisions (the so-called Assemblies of the Land), there was no voting. Truth was sought by a lengthy process of mutual persuasion, and it was determined when final accord was reached. While the decision of the Assembly was not legally binding on the tsar, it was morally incontestable. From this perspective, the creation of *parties*, that is, of segments or parts which fight for their *partial interests* at the expense of the other segments of the people, seems an absurdity. (Indeed this is less than worthy of mankind, at least of mankind in its potential.)

It is no accident that the powerful regime before which the free world trembles (including the free Western leaders, legislators, and journalists) has made no effort more concentrated and ferocious in sixty years than its attempt to eradicate Christianity—the world view of its subjugated country. And yet they have proved incapable of destroying it!

And at this time the latest informants hasten to persuade the West that this ever-vital Christianity is in fact the greatest danger.

9.

Some Words of Explanation

Any public statement with social or political overtones always elicits a great deal of comment, much of it sober and scrupulous, but the distorted reactions are invariably the loudest, they acquire hysterical headlines and attempt to imprint themselves on the memory, not without occasional success. My way of life, my work habits, and principles of behavior usually preclude any response on my part to all this cacophony. But now that I have touched upon some issues of consequence, I would like very briefly to comment on a number of distortions.

Apropos of my *Letter to the Soviet Leaders* and on other occasions since then, I have been repeatedly charged with being an advocate of a theocratic state, a system in which the government would be under the direct control of religious leaders. This is a flagrant misrepresentation; I have never said or written anything of the sort. The day-to-day activity of governing in no sense belongs to the sphere of religion. What I do believe is that the state should not persecute religion, and that, furthermore, religion should make an appropriate contribution to the spiritual life of the nation. Such a situation obtains in Poland and Israel and no one condemns it; I cannot understand why the same thing should be forbidden to Russia—a land that has carried its faith through ten centuries and earned the right to it by sixty years of suffering and the blood of millions of laymen and tens of thousands of clergy.

At the same time I was accused of propounding some kind of "way back"; one must think a man a fool to ascribe to him the desire to move against the flow of time. It was alleged that I am asking the future Russia "to renounce modern technology." Another fabrication: I had in fact called for "highly developed technology," albeit "on a small, non-gigantic scale."

The path that I do propose is set forth in the conclusion of my Harvard speech and I can repeat it here: there is no other way left but—*upward*. I believe that the lavishly materialistic twentieth century has all too long kept us in a sub-human state—some of us through superabundance, others through hunger.

The Harvard speech rewarded me with an outpouring of favorable responses from the American public at large (some of these found their way into newspapers). For that reason I was not perturbed by the outburst of reproaches that an angry press rained down upon me. I had not expected it to be so unreceptive to criticism: I was called a fanatic, a man possessed, a mind split apart, a cynic, a vindictive warmonger; I was even simply told to "get out of the country" (a fine way of applying the principle of free speech, but hardly distinguishable from Soviet practice). There were indignant questions about how I dare use the phrase "our country" in reference to the one that banished me. (The point of course is that the communist government, not Russia, had deported me.) Richard Pipes brought up the "freedom of speech which so annoys Solzhenitsyn." In fact, it was stated plainly enough for all who can read that I had in mind not freedom of speech, but only the irresponsible and amoral abuse of this freedom.

But the most widespread allegation was that I "call upon the West" to liberate our people from the communists. This could not have been said by anyone who had made a conscientious effort to read and comprehend the text. I have never made any such appeal either in my Harvard address or at any time before that, indeed never once in all my public statements over the years have I appealed for help to a single Western government or parliament. I have always maintained that we shall liberate *ourselves*, that it is *our own* task, difficult as it may be. To the West I have made but one request and offered but one word of advice. First the request: please do not force us into the grip of dictatorship, do not betray millions of our countrymen as you did in 1945, and do not use your technological resources to further strengthen our oppressors. And the advice: take care lest your headlong retreat lead you into a pit from which there is no climbing out.

After the Harvard speech, some members of the press asked with feigned surprise how I could defend the "right not to know." As a rule, they cut the quotation short, omitting: "not to have their divine souls stuffed with gossip, nonsense, vain talk." My answer is already expressed in that omitted passage. They pointed out reproachfully that this is the same Solzhenitsyn who when in the U.S.S.R. struggled for the right *to know*. Yes, I did struggle for the right of the whole world to know—about the Gulag Archipelago, about the popular resistance to communism, about the millions of dead, about the famine of 1933 and the treachery of 1945. But we who have lived through these grim years are pained when the press offers us gratuitous details about a former British Prime Minister who has undergone surgery on one testicle, about the kind of blanket Jacqueline Kennedy uses, or about the favorite drink of some female pop star.

A more serious misunderstanding arose from the passage where I said that the deadly crush of life in the East has developed greater depth of character than the well-ordered life of the West. Some bewildered commentators interpreted this as praise for the virtues of communism and an assertion of the spiritual superiority of the Soviet system. Of course I meant no such thing. This is no more than the ancient truth that strength of character comes from suffering and adversity. Oppressed and driven as they are by constant poverty, it is inevitable that many of our people are crushed, debased, warped, or dehumanized. But evil that bears down openly upon men corrupts less insidiously than does the furtive, seductive variety of evil. Direct oppression can give birth to a contrary process too—a process of spiritual ascent, even of soaring flight. Russian faces seldom if ever wear a token smile, but we are more generous in our support of one another. This is all done voluntarily and informally, and such sacrifices are in no sense tax deductible; indeed no such system even exists in our country. Taking risks for the sake of others is part of the moral climate in which we live, and I have more than once had occasion to witness the transformation which people from the West have undergone after living and working for a long period in Soviet conditions. It was reported that one American reader had offered his daughters one hundred dollars each to read the second volume of *The Gulag Archipelago*—but that the girls had refused. In our country, on the other hand, people read it even under threat of imprisonment. Or compare two young people—one a cowardly terrorist in Western Europe turning his bombs against peaceful citizens and a democratic government, the other a dissident in Eastern Europe stepping forth with bare hands against the dragon of communism. Compare, too, young Americans anxious to avoid the draft with the young Soviet soldiers who refused to fire upon insurgents—in Berlin, in Budapest, or in Afghanistan—and who were summarily executed (as they knew they would be!).

I can envision no salvation for mankind other than through the universal exercise of self-limitation by individuals and peoples alike. That is the spirit which imbues the religious and national renascence currently under way in Russia. It is something that I put forward as my fundamental belief in an essay entitled "Repentance and Self-Limitation in the Life of Nations," published five years ago in America.[18] For some reason, my opponents avoid mentioning this essay or quoting from it.

Not long ago *The New York Review of Books* carried a prominent and ominous headline: "The Dangers of Solzhenitsyn's Nationalism." But neither the journal nor its infor-

[18] In *From Under the Rubble* (Boston-Toronto: Little, Brown, 1975).

mants had the wit to indicate in the essay thus advertised where exactly these dangers lay. Well, then, I shall help them out with some quotations from my published writings.

From my *Letter to the Soviet Leaders:*[19]

"I wish all people well, and the closer they are to us and the more dependent upon us, the more fervent is my wish." (p. 7)

"One aches with sympathy for the ordinary Chinese too, because it is they who will be the most helpless victims of the war." (p. 16)

From my essay on "Repentance and Self-Limitation" in *From Under the Rubble:*

"We shall have to find in ourselves the resolve . . . to acknowledge our *external* sins, those against other peoples." (p. 128)

"With regard to all the peoples in and beyond our borders forcibly drawn into our orbit, we can fully purge our guilt [only] by giving them genuine freedom to decide their future for themselves." (p. 135)

"Just as it is impossible to build a good society when relations between people are bad, there will never be a good world while nations are on bad terms and secretly cherish the desire for revenge. . . . Among states too the moral rule for individuals will be adopted—do not unto others as you would not have done unto you." (pp. 134, 137)

So there you have the danger of "Solzhenitsyn's nationalism." This is the threat of the Russian religious and national revival.

[19] Aleksandr Solzhenitsyn, *Letter to the Soviet Leaders* (New York: Harper & Row, 1974).

10.

One Step from the Brink

Today Afghanistan, yesterday Czechoslovakia and Angola, tomorrow some other Soviet takeover—yet even after all this, how good it would be to go on believing in détente! Could it really be over? "But the Soviet leaders haven't repudiated it at all! Brezhnev was quite clear about that: it was in *Pravda!*" (Thus Marshall Shulman and other, like-minded experts.)

Yes indeed, the Soviet leaders are quite prepared to carry on détente; why shouldn't they be? This is the same détente that the West basked in so contentedly while millions were being exterminated in the jungles of Cambodia. The same détente that so gladdened Western hearts at a time when a thousand men, including twelve-year-old boys, were being executed in one Afghan village. (And this was surely not a unique case!) We Russians immediately recognize an episode like this. That's the Soviet way of doing things! That's the way they slaughtered us, too, from 1918 on! Détente will continue to stand Soviet communism in very good stead: for the purpose of stifling the last flicker of dissidence in the Soviet Union and buying up whatever electronic equipment is necessary.

The West simply does not want to believe that the time for sacrifices has arrived; it is simply unprepared for sacrifices. Men who go on trading right until the first salvo is fired are incapable of sacrificing so much as their commercial profits: they have not the wit to realize that their children will never enjoy these gains, that today's illusory profits will return as tomorrow's devastation. The Western allies are maneuvering to see who can sacrifice the least. Behind all this lies that sleek god of affluence, now proclaimed as the goal of life, replacing the high-minded view of the world which the West has lost.

Communism will never be halted by negotiations or through the machinations of détente. It can be halted only by force from without or by disintegration from within. The smooth and effortless course of the West's long retreat could not go on forever, and it is now coming to an end; the brink may not have been reached, but it is already the merest step away. Since the outlying borders were never defended, the nearer ones will have to be held. Today the Western world faces a greater danger than that which threatened it in 1939.

It would be disastrous for the world if America were to look upon the Peking leadership as an ally while regarding the Russian people as no less a foe than communism: by so doing she would drive both these great nations into the maw of communism and plunge in after them. She would deprive both great peoples of their last hope of liberation. The indefatigable denigrators of Russia and all things Russian are forgetting to check their watches: All of America's mistakes and misconceptions about Russia might have been purely academic in the past, but not in the swift-moving world of today. On the eve of the global battle between world communism and world humanity, would that the West at least distinguished the enemies of humanity from its friends, and that it sought an alliance not of foes but of friends. So much has been ceded, surrendered, and traded away that today even a fully united Western world can no longer prevail except by allying itself with the captive peoples of the communist world.

Vermont
February 1980

Mr. Solzhenitsyn and His Critics

The following letters appeared in *Foreign Affairs* in response
to *The Mortal Danger.*

To the Editor:

Aleksandr Solzhenitsyn's article, "Misconceptions about
Russia Are a Threat to America" [*The Mortal Danger*], in
Foreign Affairs (Spring 1980) is written in the acrimonious
and disdainful tone of a person who desires to discredit those
who think differently, myself included, rather than open a
dialogue with them. I do not intend to reply in kind. My
purpose is to show why I consider Mr. Solzhenitsyn's basic
view of communism unsound, to give the readers of *Foreign
Affairs* a clearer picture than he did of the article of mine that
he criticized and the important issues involved, and, of
course, to answer his criticisms.

The Marxist movement that came to be called "communism" arose in Russia early in this century under Lenin's leadership and was then called "bolshevism." Mr. Solzhenitsyn's
basic view is that there is not and never was anything specifically Russian about communism; that communism and Russia
do not mix, save as a cancerous tumor mixes with the body on

75

which it lethally preys; and that the same applies to communism in relation to any other nation to which it has spread or may spread. Communism is non-national and anti-national. It is fundamentally uniform and changeless. It undergoes no serious alterations either across frontiers or over time, e.g., as between communist-ruled Russia under Lenin and under Stalin.

That being Mr. Solzhenitsyn's basic view, one can readily see why he was incensed by my article "Stalin, the Last Bolshevik." Printed in *The New York Times* on December 21, 1979, the one hundredth anniversary of Stalin's birth, it asserted that bolshevism was an inwardly diverse movement in Lenin's time and that what Stalin represented was only one current within it, albeit the current that prevailed. The article characterized Stalin's current as "Russian national bolshevism: a blend of Leninist Marxism and Russian nationalism." Given his basic position that communism and Russia do not mix, that communism and nationalism are antithetical phenomena, Mr. Solzhenitsyn cannot imagine the possibility of such a (mixed) phenomenon as "Russian national bolshevism." It would be a contradiction in terms. So, he finds it "astounding" that a scholar and student of politics like myself could persist to this day in "misunderstanding so fundamentally the phenomenon of communism," i.e., in differing so fundamentally from *his* view of it. It will explain why I differ.

Mr. Solzhenitsyn is mistaken in thinking that communism and national cultures are necessarily in all ways antithetical, and also in regarding communism as essentially uniform and changeless in nature. A large body of historical evidence exists to show: (1) that communism as an ideology, social order and form of rule, while always authoritarian within the frame of the single-party state, often assimilates, or blends in subtle ways, with various elements of national cultural tradition in countries where communist parties come to power, so that an amalgam of communism and national culture is formed; (2)

that communism therefore tends to differ somewhat in character from country to country, e.g., as between Russia and Yugoslavia or Russia and China, because their national pasts differ; and (3) that communism, notably in the first communist-ruled country, Russia, has undergone very significant changes from period to period: from Lenin's time to Stalin's, from Stalin's to Khrushchev's, and from Khrushchev's to Brezhnev's.

For example, Mr. Solzhenitsyn's story about life in a Stalinist concentration camp, *One Day in the Life of Ivan Denisovich,* would not have been published (or its author freed from exile) in Stalin's Russia, would not be publishable in Brezhnev's Russia of today, but was published in Khrushchev's Russia in the Soviet literary journal *Novy Mir;* and the writer of that excellent work will be aware of the very great significance, and not for him alone, of this particular change in Russia's communism over time. Examples could easily be multiplied manyfold. In the West, a whole new field, "comparative communist studies," has arisen in the recent past as scholars have grasped the need to take these differences into account and to analyze their nature and causes. Mr. Solzhenitsyn's vision of a changeless internationalist communism that does not and and cannot amalgamate with elements of national cultures is simply an extreme version of a position that dominated Western studies of communism, to their detriment, at an earlier time and has been overcome slowly as more open-minded scholars in the field pondered factual evidence and its meaning.

But the issue is not between a Russian way of thinking about communism (Solzhenitsyn's) and a Western way (the newer historical, cultural, and comparative approach). The idea, so unacceptable to Mr. Solzhenitsyn, that Russia and communism could and did blend to form an amalgam in Lenin's Bolshevik movement has never been better stated than it was by Nicolas Berdyaev, a thinker whose Russian national, Rus-

77

sian Orthodox religious, and non-communist credentials were at least as strong as his. That well-known Russian emigré opened his book, *The Origin of Russian Communism* (London: Saunders, 1937), with these true and memorable words:

> Russian Communism is difficult to understand on account of its twofold nature. On the one hand it is international and a world phenomenon; on the other hand it is national and Russian. It is particularly important for Western minds to understand the national roots of Russian Communism and the fact that it was Russian history which determined its limits and shaped its character.

Berdyaev saw that there were subtle, distinctively Russian traits in bolshevism even before it took power in 1917, such as a fierce, utterly intolerant insistence on orthodoxy (Lenin's version of Marxism), an acrimonious style of discourse that very often sought to discredit those who believed differently, and a messianic spirit that had national antecedents in old Muscovy's ideological conception of itself as the only Orthodox tsardom, the "Third Rome."

In *The Russian Idea* (London: Macmillan, 1947, p. 250), Berdyaev said further that there "took place a sharp nationalization of Soviet Russia and a return to many traditions of the Russian past. Leninism and Stalinism are not classical Marxism. . . . Communism is a Russian phenomenon in spite of its Marxist ideology." Were he alive and writing now, Berdyaev would very likely amend that statement to read that communism, having been transplanted to China, Yugoslavia, Hungary, etc., has tended to become in those countries, despite its Soviet Russian origin, a Chinese communist, Yugoslav communist, Hungarian communist phenomenon, etc., while still preserving some general features that differing communisms have in common (the party-state structure, for example, and allegiance to the idea of "Marxism-Leninism" as a guiding

78

creed, along with significant differences in ways of interpreting what that creed means). And he would be right in taking such a view. Between his mind and Mr. Solzhenitsyn's there is no less a chasm than there is between that of a Western scholar like myself and Mr. Solzhenitsyn's. Hence we are not dealing with an issue that pits Russian against foreigner. Mr. Solzhenitsyn is in no position to lecture the American and world public on *the Russian* view of things. His is one influential Russian's view, shared by some people in his homeland and abroad, not shared by others.

My article about Stalin argued that he combined bolshevism with Russian nationalism in a very special way. The particular element of the Russian national past that he found highly relevant to the problems of the Soviet Russian present was the early tsarist and imperial tradition. He discovered in the tsarist heritage of earlier centuries—the fifteenth to the eighteenth—a model of forced national development for creating a strong military state in a hostile international encirclement. In particular, he found in the policies of Tsar Peter I, whom the nineteenth-century Russian thinker Alexander Herzen called "a revolutionary, albeit a crowned one," a Russian ruler whose example he could and did take as a model in the "revolution from above" that he led in the internationally isolated Soviet Russia of the early 1930s. He thus reshaped Soviet communism in the direction of a Soviet Russian imperial communism, in which the international communist revolution was equated with the aggrandizement of the Soviet Russian state.

When confronted with criticism by many Old Bolsheviks in the early 1930s, mainly because of the catastrophic famine that resulted from his misguided effort to drive the peasants into collectives by terror, so that the state could take possession of large amounts of grain to export for financing the forced industrialization program, Stalin reacted with fury and carried through in 1934–39 a gigantic terroristic purge of the

Soviet Communist Party. In this he took as his model another, still earlier Russian ruler, Tsar Ivan IV, whose terroristic purge of *his* higher aristocracy in the sixteenth century helped cause him to go down in Russia's history as "Ivan the Terrible."

Mr. Solzhenitsyn is pained. He states: "Professor Tucker hastens to salvage socialism by suggesting that Stalin was not, after all, a *genuine* socialist! He did not act in accordance with Marxist theories, but trod in the footsteps of that wearisome pair, Ivan the Terrible from the sixteenth century and Peter the Great from the eighteenth." That statement twists and distorts the clear message of my article, which said that many people abroad "overlooked the persisting Bolshevik elements in Stalin's amalgam of bolshevism and Russian nationalism, mistaking him for a national leader whose obeisances to socialism and Marxism were ideological verbiage. Stalin never forsook socialism and Marxism in his understanding of them: socialism was the state-dominated system of society being formed in his revolution from above; Marxism was the doctrine that sanctified such a system as socialist."

As for the "wearisome pair," Mr. Solzhenitsyn is free to be wearied by whatever wearies him, but the question is whether Stalin in fact chose to emulate the action patterns of those two Russian rulers (in his understanding of them). If he did—and I have sought to adduce evidence on this in various published writings and a further book yet to appear—then no one has a right to deny the historical significance of Stalin's attitude toward those tsars on the ground of the theme's tiresomeness.

As if recognizing this, Mr. Solzhenitsyn steps back and asks, "Just what 'model' could Stalin have seen in the former, tsarist Russia, as Tucker has it? Camps there were none; the very concept was unknown." Before commenting on this inaccuracy, I must point out that the question of Stalin's revival of tsarist patterns and practices cannot be reduced to the matter of camps, nor can the tsarist political tradition be equated—as Mr. Solzhenitsyn proceeds to do in his article— with the relatively liberalized tsarist state system of the old regime's final period. The tsarist patterns that Stalin found worthy of emulation in his policies lay more in the distant Russian past. One such pattern was serfdom, the attachment of the peasant to the land, and, associated with it, *barshchina* (the *corvée*); these were resurrected, save in name, in the Stalinist "collective farm" and the legislation of the latter 1930s concerning its operative procedures. Another pattern was the system of ranks, uniforms and insignia for state officials that Stalin recreated on the model of the one established by Tsar Peter with his "Table of Ranks."

Despite his preference for precedents from "progressive" (as they were officially called in Stalin's Russia) tsars like Ivan III in the fifteenth century, who forged the centralized Great Russian state system, Ivan IV in the sixteenth, and Peter I in the eighteenth, Stalin was not above taking a few leaves from books of very late tsars. In 1932, in order to control the places of residence and movements of people in Soviet Russia, he resurrected the internal passport system that had existed in tsarist Russia right up to 1917 and been abolished by the revolution. In 1934, he established in his internal affairs commissariat a "special board" with a composition and powers (of administrative exile for up to five years of elements deemed dangerous by the authorities) that reproduced those of the "special board" set up in the tsarist internal affairs ministry following the assassination of Tsar Alexander II in 1881. Stalin was personally well acquainted with the earlier "special board," having repeatedly been sent away by its order in his years as a revolutionary. The ease with which he made his several escapes may have inspired the measures he took to tighten the penal system while expanding it enormously.

Now as to camps. Forced-labor camps of the kind that mushroomed in Soviet Russia from 1929 onward had no comparable counterpart in tsarist Russia. But Mr. Solzhenitsyn, who has found their beginnings in the concentration camps that were set up on Lenin's authority in 1918 as the Russian civil war began, to imprison opponents of the Bolshevik regime and not for forced labor, needs to pursue his historical research further. When he does, he will find that governmental use of forced labor existed in tsarist Russia, notably under the rule of tiresome Tsar Peter, who not only attached whole serf villages to newly built Russian war factories but brought together prisoners of war, civilians from occupied territories, and state-owned serfs in what a noted economic historian of Anglo-Russian upbringing and wide Russian experience, Leonard Hubbard, called "Peter's forced-labor camps" for canal construction and the like.[1] Forced labor was also used in the building of Peter's new capital on northern marshland, and "camp" might possibly be a fair description of the conditions in which the forced laborers were housed—if they were.

But Mr. Solzhenitsyn need not look so far into the past to find a tsarist pedigree for the Soviet forced-labor camps. He need only consult the record of a journey taken in 1885–86, from the Urals eastward and back, by George Kennan, an uncle of our contemporary, George Frost Kennan, on whose distinguished career as an interpreter of Soviet Russia to America Mr. Solzhenitsyn has unwarrantedly cast aspersion in the same *Foreign Affairs* essay. Admittedly, the very fact that Kennan was allowed to take that trip and observe convict laborers at work is a point in favor of the state system in late tsarist Russia compared with that in Soviet Russia. He devoted a long chapter of his meticulous record of observations to the conditions he witnessed in the convict gold mines of Eastern Siberia. They belonged to the tsar and brought him an annual yield of 3,600 pounds of pure gold in return for an outlay of

[1]Leonard Hubbard, *The Economics of Soviet Agriculture* (London: Macmillan, 1939), p. 19.

500,000 rubles, or about $250,000, for maintaining the penal mining establishment. A representative passage from Kennan's subsequently published account of his journey is worth quoting:

> On one side of an open square, around which stood the prison and the barracks, forty or fifty convicts in long gray overcoats with yellow diamonds on their backs were at work upon a new log building, surrounded by a cordon of Cossacks in sheepskin *shubas,* felt boots, and muff-shaped fur caps, who stood motionless at their posts, leaning upon their Berdan rifles and watching the prisoners.[2]

A small-scale affair, as was the whole convict-labor gold-mining operation in Eastern Siberia, by comparison with the vast forced-labor empire built in Stalin's time; and those gray overcoats were doubtless much better protection against the cold than the miserable garments issued to convict laborers in Soviet Russia. Otherwise, however, the scene bears some resemblance to scenes that have been graphically described by Mr. Solzhenitsyn in his book, *The Gulag Archipelago.* The real point, moreover, is that the forced-labor system in Soviet Russia had antecedents, and thus precedents, in tsarist Russia.

Mr. Solzhenitsyn writes that modesty prevents him from asking me to read at least the first volume of *The Gulag Archipelago,* and better still all three. Modesty does not prevent me from revealing that I have read all three. I have learned much from them about experiences in the Soviet camps, adding to all I previously learned from other valuable works on this subject. What surprises me is that Mr. Solzhenitsyn seems to believe that Western scholarship had neglected or even hushed up this subject prior to the appearance of his opus. This is, quite simply, inaccurate. Here are the titles of two

[2]George Kennan, *Siberia and the Exile System* (abridged) (Chicago: University of Chicago Press, 1958), p. 171.

most carefully researched and richly informative volumes familiar to all serious scholars in Soviet studies: David J. Dallin and Boris I. Nicolaevsky, *Forced Labor in Soviet Russia* (New Haven: Yale University Press, 1947), and S. Swianiewicz, *Forced Labour and Economic Development: An Enquiry into the Experience of Soviet Industrialization* (London: Oxford University Press, 1965). To them must be added numerous highly informative firsthand accounts, such as Elinor Lipper's *Eleven Years in Soviet Prison Camps* (Chicago: Henry Regnery Co., 1951) and Jerzy Gliksman's *Tell the West: An Account of His Experiences as a Slave Laborer in the Union of Soviet Socialist Republics* (New York: Gresham Press, 1948), to mention only two outstanding examples among the far larger number that might be given.

There is a further problem. For all the mass of important testimony that it contains, *The Gulag Archipelago* does a disservice to historical understanding by compressing the factual material into the author's simplistic, straight-line scheme of Soviet development, a scheme that treats all the horrors of the Stalin era as the logical and necessary unfolding of what was embryonic in Lenin's communism from the start. From this standpoint, there *was* no distinct Stalin era, and the very word "Stalinism" is taboo. In the portion of his *Foreign Affairs* essay devoted to my article, Mr. Solzhenitsyn makes that conclusion quite explicit: "No 'Stalinism' has ever existed, either in theory or in practice; there was never any such phenomenon or any such era. This concept was invented after 1956 by intellectuals of the European Left as a way of salvaging the 'ideals' of communism." And further: "In the Soviet Union it used to be said with good reason that 'Stalin is Lenin today' . . ."

It used to be Stalin who wanted people to say and believe that, believed it himself, and never allowed the term "Stalinism" to be introduced into Soviet official usage. It is ironic, and ultimately sad, that the ex-Soviet Russian Army officer who was started on his long trek through Gulag in 1945 because of an incautious critical allusion to Stalin in a private letter to a friend, and who must have known then that Stalin was hardly "Lenin today," should wind up now, in conditions of freedom thirty-five years after, repeating as solemn truth what the infinitely arrogant, self-adulating Stalin thought of himself.

Because he grew up in ignorance of many important developments owing to Soviet censorship practices, Mr. Solzhenitsyn may be forgiven for not knowing that the concept "Stalinism" was developed not by European intellectuals circa 1956 but by Bolshevik oppositionists of the late 1920s and early 1930s. That is a side issue, as is the question whether we really require the term "Stalinism" for the era of Soviet history over which Stalin presided and the distinctive sociopolitical formation that he fathered—or, as I prefer, "Russian national bolshevism." The real and vital issue is whether, as I believe and believe historical evidence bears out, there was such an era and such a formation, or whether, as Mr. Solzhenitsyn believes, there was not.

This is not, as it might seem, an argument over history alone. It affects our way of understanding trends and events in today's Soviet Russia. If Stalin's current in the Soviet communist movement was one that blended bolshevism with Russian nationalism, then we will not—like Mr. Solzhenitsyn—be blind to the possibility that a most malignant form of extreme Russian nationalism may be germinating, or fully germinated, in certain Soviet circles of our time. That would be an expectable part of Stalin's legacy, a form of Russian chauvinism with only the thinnest veneer of bolshevism left on it, if that. We would see the invasion and brutal military occupation of Afghanistan as the act of Soviet Russian imperialism that it appears to have been—again, in keeping with Stalin's legacy to Soviet Russia as a leader who combined bolshevism with the imperial Russian tradition and thereby fashioned a system and a foreign policy embodying the worst features of both.

On one point, Mr. Solzhenitsyn and I are in complete agreement: misconceptions about Russia are dangerous. Unfortunately, his own mind, as manifested in his article for *Foreign Affairs,* is far from free of them.

ROBERT C. TUCKER
Princeton University

Princeton, N.J.
Summer 1980

To the Editor:

I am too insignificant a citizen to presume to write to you for publication. I do venture to think, however, that as a subscriber, as an assiduous reader, and as a warm admirer of *Foreign Affairs,* I may express to its editor my dismay that no less than thirty-seven pages are given to Mr. Solzhenitsyn for what is, essentially, a disparaging and abusive tirade against the American people. We are treated as benighted blunderers, bumblers and ignorants, ill informed by incompetent diplomats and unobservant foreign correspondents, and—to top it all—as biased in favor of communism. If this were not enough, he is also guilty of a most transparent attempt to sow disunity among various groups of our people.

As a not universally welcome guest of these selfsame ill-informed Americans, he lectures us as he would a bunch of errant children (or worse), and is unsparingly abusive of our political actions and of our political thinking. Yet he, himself, is so arrogantly biased that he absolves nineteenth-century Russia of any crime of violence, repression or persecution. Has he never heard of pogroms or just doesn't he care? And what of the oh-so-pacific and benign expansionism of nineteenth-century tsarist Russia!

Mr. Solzhenitsyn and His Critics

Foreign Affairs rightly offers the hospitality of its pages to all viewpoints, but when a foreign guest writes as patronizingly and one-sidedly as Mr. Solzhenitsyn, some words of instant rebuttal seem a much needed response to his bad manners. This is particularly true when a man of acknowledged literary stature, a Nobel laureate at that, steps off his pedestal to berate his hosts.

I know that this letter of mine is not a rebuttal in any sense of the word. It is merely the angry, off-the-cuff reaction of a reader who had sincerely hoped that the Harvard speech was enough abuse for us to swallow from this most unappreciative visitor.

SILVIO J. TREVES

New York, N.Y.
Summer 1980

To the Editor:

Aleksandr Solzhenitsyn's article, "Misconceptions about Russia Are a Threat to America" [*The Mortal Danger*], in your Spring 1980 issue contains a number of factual errors which, coupled with the author's intense biases, deny any validity to his argument. Part of what he has to say is important, for instance, on the necessity to distinguish between the U.S.S.R. and Russia. However, if Mr. Solzhenitsyn's advice were followed in the United States, it would preclude a coherent policy toward the Soviet Union.

Mr. Solzhenitsyn makes errors about virtually every aspect of Imperial Russian history he mentions. He writes that "all criminal investigations were conducted in strict compliance with established law, all trials were open and defendants were legally represented." Hardly: instead, the "Extraordinary Measures" of 1881 gave provincial governors and other local officials power to hold closed trials or transfer cases to military courts whenever this was necessary "to protect public order and calm." The vagueness is typical of tsarist law, which was justly famous for its arbitrariness as well. Particularly after the 1905 Revolution, thousands of peasants and workers were tried by military court martial and condemned to death. As for criminal investigations, they were often bypassed in favor of quick administrative action, especially in political cases. By 1912 only five million Russians did *not* live under one of the Extraordinary Measures; they were the real constitution of the country, as Richard Pipes has pointed out.

"The intelligentsia was not restricted in its activity." In fact, the organizations of the intelligentsia, for example doctors' and teachers' groups, were under constant surveillance by tsarist police, public lectures were often banned because of political content, journals were shut down, and all levels of education were carefully monitored and regulated by the state. By 1914 there were many, many signs of severe discontent with tsarism among the Russian intelligentsia.

"Institutions of higher education enjoyed inviolable autonomy." On the contrary, it was only because the regime was forced to the wall by the events of 1905 that it granted (more precisely, regranted) autonomy to the universities; yet within a few years tsarist ministers of education had once again begun to interfere deeply in university affairs. The most notorious case involved Moscow University in 1911, when the current minister sent police onto the campus and fired the rector. The result was that more than one hundred faculty members resigned in protest. In other higher educational institutions, for example Moscow's municipal university, state interference was less spectacular but nonetheless regular and effective.

"Religious and philosophical views of every shade were tolerated." The case of the Jews alone refutes this point, though other examples could be offered: perhaps their religious views were "tolerated," but the Jewish people were largely restricted to a certain geographical area, were subject to narrow quotas in admission to the universities, and were sometimes the victims of officially condoned or sponsored pogroms. This is hardly a progressive religious policy.

When he turns to the Soviet Union, Mr. Solzhenitsyn's accuracy does not improve. He states that "Soviet conquerors never withdraw from any lands on which they have once set foot." On the contrary, there are at least four examples of Soviet withdrawal: after World War II from part of Finland, northern Iran and Manchuria; in 1956 from the U.S.S.R.'s sector of Austria.

The point of this recital of his errors is not to show that tsarist Russia was "bad" and the Soviet Union is "good," for that would be a tragic perversion of history. In many ways, of course, Mr. Solzhenitsyn's belief that the old regime was better than the Bolshevik state is justified. The communist government has allowed far less freedom of expression and religion, used far more coercion and slaughtered people on a scale far greater than the tsars ever dreamed of. But these judgments are of virtually no help in understanding the Russian empire and its fate or in fathoming the Soviet Union today.

American scholars have long conducted a lively debate over the question of "whither Russia on the eve of the First World War," democratic evolution or revolution? Was it largely the devastating effects of the war which led to tsardom's collapse or was it mroe the result of long-standing, deeply rooted forces?

For Mr. Solzhenitsyn, there is no debate, no doubt about the reasons for Russia's downfall. "She collapsed out of loyalty to her Western allies, when Nicholas II prolonged the senseless war with Wilhelm instead of saving his country." But one must ask how could two and a half years of combat destroy loyalties so quickly that in February 1917, during riots in the capital, all of the front-line army commanders refused to support the Emperor? Not even the conservative politicians rallied to help Nicholas. The country's disaffection included the *institutions* of tsarism: there was almost no positive response to Nicholas' proposals that his son, and later his brother, take the throne. Russians wanted an end to the system they had lived under for centuries.

In *From Under the Rubble,* Mr. Solzhenitsyn recognizes that the eight months of 1917 from the fall of the monarchy to the Bolshevik takeover constitute the only period of democracy Russia has known. He does not go on to say that the trend away from tsarism was so strong that by the end of that time the question which dominated politics, which occupied the thoughts of the vast majority of Russians, was what form of socialism the country should adopt. In elections held in the fall of 1917 to choose delegates for the Constituent Assembly, socialists of various parties won over 87 percent of the vote. Thus the Russians, at their freest according to Mr. Solzhenitsyn, moved in a direction which is anathema to him.

It seems to me that Mr. Solzhenitsyn is no better in touch with the Soviet present than he is with the Russian past. I recently spent ten months doing research in the U.S.S.R., where I had many opportunities to speak with people at various levels of society. As part of an exchange group, I was not subject to many of the constraints Mr. Solzhenitsyn aptly describes as hampering the ability of most Westerners to know the country in any depth. I found loyal and disloyal citizens, yet I had a strong general impression of both Russian and Soviet patriotism. The other participants in the program, whose political views spanned a wide range, largely agreed. Among the reasons for this patriotism are the government-sponsored but genuinely popular cult of the Second World War, official and popular fear of the United States, a much greater fear of China, and awareness of the many past inva-

sions of the country. I also noted a widespread pride in the
material progress the Soviet Union has made; the people's
basis of comparison for this feeling is, of course, tsarist Russia.
I believe that for many Soviets these factors balance to a fair
degree the many negative aspects of their lives.

From my experience in the U.S.S.R. and my study of Russian and Soviet history, I must conclude that an appeal by the
United States to Russian national sentiment within the Soviet
Union might meet with some covert sympathy but would be
angrily resented by most citizens, Russians and non-Russians
alike, as crude interference in their affairs. The need for a
strong country, perceived by many Soviet people, means
sticking together.

ROBERT W. THURSTON
Visiting Assistant Professor
of History
The University of Vermont

Burlington, Vermont
Fall 1980

To the Editor:

I am afraid that the real misconception about Russia, which
I believe is a threat to America, lies with Aleksandr Solzhenitsyn. If we would accept his conception about Russia and try
to derive an adequate foreign policy from it, we would do the
greatest service to the Soviet Union and the greatest disservice to the United States.

For this particular danger, that is, Russian imperialism, it is
not at all politically relevant how anyone perceives Russia or
the history of Russia and the discussion could be left to historians.

No doubt anyone should feel respect and admiration for the

"spiritual life of the Russian people and its view of the world —Christianity." However, these and similar features of the Russian people are not proof that there does not exist a real Russian imperialism, which today is the great danger to our civilization. As a matter of fact this Russian imperialism entered the scene of world politics after the Second World War to replace the German Nazi imperialism.

We are entitled to speak of German Nazism and imperialism though we have no right to disregard the "spiritual life" of the German people and "its view of the world—Christianity." For many years the German nation was regarded as the nation of poets and thinkers and gave the world even more and greater thinkers, scientists, poets and musicians than Russia. Nevertheless Nazism was German and very specifically German. Fortunately after the defeat of Hitler in Germany, many German thinkers, politicians, writers, poets, etc., did recognize the German role in Nazism and tried together with ordinary people and particularly with the young generations of Germany to create a new Germany. While condemning not only Nazism but also its historical roots in the German nation, we should not accept the concept of collective guilt, just as we should give full support and credibility for all anti-Nazi and humanistic efforts that appeal to the better traditions of Germany, while the Hitlerites appealed to its worst traditions. However, these worst traditions did exist and were German.

The same applies to Russia. There is no doubt that there existed a Russian imperialism and Russia was regarded and called the "gendarme of Europe," being the most reactionary government at the turn of the century and the ally of all oppressive governments. Russian imperialism had its specific features as it emerged from an Asiatic feudalism typical of tsarist Russia. The tsarist dream of world domination caught the soul of the Russian nation and, unfortunately, survived to become even more pronounced under the rule of Russian communism, which also has its typical Russian features, just as the Chinese version of communism has its Chinese features and the Yugoslav communism its Yugoslav features.

Strangely, Mr. Solzhenitsyn himself shows that Russia is to blame for what the Soviet Union stands for when he speaks about the historically proven fact that the Ukrainians, and for that matter the Baltic nations, welcomed the Nazi invaders, and the Ukrainians were particularly willing to join the German Nazis in their fight against the Soviets. Thanks to the Nazis' arrogance and their belief that they were a superior nation, however, Hitler did not accept the Ukrainians as allies and treated them as subhumans. For this blunder Hitler most probably lost the war against the Soviet Union; many military experts agree that he might have been able to enter Moscow and subdue the Soviets.

On the other hand, when German armies entered Russia proper, the Russian people did not act like the Ukrainians. In 1946 Stalin was perfectly right when he evaluated the situation and declared that no other nation but the Russian nation was willing to make such fantastic sacrifices and had the will to fight and defeat the German invader. He thus admitted that only the Russian nation identified its national interest with the Soviet Union. This manifestation of Russian nationalism was a component of the old Russian imperialist tradition.

If we want to fight Soviet imperialism, we must be aware that the majority of the states in the Soviet Union are oppressed nations, more than simply oppressed individuals. They exist as discriminated nations: the economy is run from Moscow according to interests that are first of all Russian interests. Russian culture and language is the preferred one all over the Soviet Union. Between these nations and the Russians exists an explosive tension.

As we know, the problem of suppressed or discriminated nations is an explosive political force even in democratic countries. We see this problem in Canada, Britain, Spain, etc., and it exists naturally in the Soviet Union. It is therefore necessary to fight the Soviet Union by emphasizing the issue of self-determination of nations, to find ways and means to support the most human and humane desire of self-determination in order to weaken the Soviet hinterland, and make the Kremlin aware of an active opposition even if it does not take dramatic forms. Any increase in the resistance of the oppressed nations will weaken the military potential of the Soviets and be a contribution to peace.

I fully agree with Mr. Solzhenitsyn that the policy of détente may turn out to be the great catastrophe for the United States, and that communism, or more specifically any regime based on the Marxist philosophy, inevitably leads to a dehumanized world. The oppressed nations within the Soviet empire are potential allies of the West and particularly of the United States, and it is essential for the peace and survival of our civilization that the United States and the West should not support the oppressors in the Kremlin and its agents in Eastern Europe. The Soviet Union committed itself in the Atlantic Charter, the United Nations Charter, and at Helsinki to the right of self-determination of nations. The centerpiece of U.S. foreign policy should be the self-determination of nations.

EUGEN LOEBL

New York, N.Y.
Fall 1980

Mr. Loebl was formerly the First Deputy Minister of Foreign Trade of Czechoslovakia.

To the Editor:

In the Summer 1980 issue of *Foreign Affairs*, you printed two responses to Aleksandr Solzhenitsyn's Spring issue essay:

one by Professor Robert C. Tucker of Princeton and another by Mr. Silvio J. Treves of New York City. The responses were both so energetically hostile as to send me back to Mr. Solzhenitsyn's article, which I read carefully a second time. I think I now understand Mr. Solzhenitsyn's recurrent use of the term "astonishment" when he relates his perceptions of the West. There's no better word for it: after rereading Mr. Solzhenitsyn's article, I was astonished by the responses of Professor Tucker and of Mr. Treves.

Neither response reflects a careful reading of Mr. Solzhenitsyn's article. Professor Tucker decries in Mr. Solzhenitsyn "the acrimonious and disdainful tone of a person who desires to discredit those who think differently"—yet Professor Tucker devotes six full pages, in small type, to a rambling rebuttal aimed at less than two full pages of Mr. Solzhenitsyn's thirty-seven-page article. Professor Tucker scores a few interesting debater's points, but in one glaring and lengthy portion of his rebuttal he does so against a straw man. Professor Tucker quotes Mr. Solzhenitsyn's remark that in tsarist Russia "camps there were none" and then lectures Mr. Solzhenitsyn on the fact "that governmental use of forced labor existed in tsarist Russia"—a point which Mr. Solzhenitsyn clearly concedes on the same page of his article, when, after "camps there were none," he refers to "nonpolitical prisoners at forced labor in those days."

Nowhere in his response does Professor Tucker confront the central question raised by Mr. Solzhenitsyn's article: whether the West has indeed, particularly over the past thirty-five years, drifted into a pattern of inadvertent complicity with communist tyranny. Professor Tucker replies as if he himself and his scholarship were the sole topics of the article.

Mr. Treves, for his part, calls Mr. Solzhenitsyn "so arrogantly biased that he absolves nineteenth-century Russia of any crime of violence, repression or persecution." But Mr. Solzhenitsyn does nothing of the kind; he simply points out, correctly if bitterly, that tsarist repression was not remotely so pervasive, unrelenting, indiscriminate, or ferocious as twentieth-century Soviet brutality has been and continues to be. In fact, Mr. Treves' tirade against Mr. Solzhenitsyn's latest broadside strikes me as disingenuous. I wonder whether Mr. Treves read the article at all.

Come to think of it, how many people in the West have read Mr. Solzhenitsyn at all? I have had students in my college English classes, students with majors in history and political science, who have never heard of the Soviet Gulag. I have talked with educated people who allow that they don't read Mr. Solzhenitsyn "on principle"—by which I gather they mean on the strength of their preferred faith in the hostile articles and reviews directed against Mr. Solzhenitsyn by so many Western intellectuals. How is one to account for the strident Western reaction to Mr. Solzhenitsyn, typified by Mr. Treves' admittedly uninformed letter attributing "bad manners" to the discomfiting Russian exile? Surely the West, and especially America, is no stranger to trenchant criticism; but I don't recall a Marxist ever coming under such fire or contempt from the intellectual community as Mr. Solzhenitsyn has encountered in the West.

JOHN R. DUNLAP

San Jose, California
Fall 1980

To the Editor:

Aleksandr Solzhenitsyn's article tells us more about the author than about either Russia or America. It abounds in its own misconceptions about both countries.

I have admired Aleksandr Solzhenitsyn for his behavior in the Soviet Union, his courage, his integrity, as well as for his literary masterpieces. If it is painful to challenge his views, I do so only because to leave them unchallenged would be an even graver failing.

The essay contains its share of inaccuracies and exaggerations. More than once the author speaks of "sixty million victims" of the Soviet regime ("not counting war casualties"): we deserve to be let in on the peculiar arithmetic that yields these figures. But whether the true figure is thirteen million or thirty million, the human costs of Stalinism were terrible enough to require no inflation.

One need by no means be a sympathizer of the Soviet regime to challenge his statement that "... subsistence at such an abysmally low level—for half a century—is leading to a biological degeneration of the people that is intensified ... by the suppression of every form of culture ... where the minds of its children are systematically robbed." It does not alter my opposition to that regime one iota to recognize that in the postwar years the Soviet standard of living has gone up at a rather impressive rate; that evidence of "biological degeneration" is dubious at best; that at least the politically "safe" forms of culture are valued at least as highly as in the United States; and that public education has made significant strides.

What is at stake is not merely factual accuracy. As Aleksandr Isayevich himself states, he spent "the entire fifty-five years of [his] Soviet life in the remoter areas of the U.S.S.R." His own experience, in and out of military service and the Gulag Archipelago, thus gave him little opportunity for reliable insights into the motives and functioning of Soviet policymakers. His angle of vision is a particular one; his own truth is that of the victim, a searing truth which pervades his outlook and his values, one which he passionately translates into his apocalyptic vision. The qualities which made him a hero and a prophet are not the same qualities that are needed for political analysis or for statesmanship.

Mr. Solzhenitsyn is an ardent Russian patriot. We may ad-

97

mire him for it. But why does this patriotism require an uncritical defense of "old Russia"—the tsarist era—or, better yet, in his view, the Muscovite era prior to Peter the Great, before Russia was contaminated by the "corrupting" West? Why not admit that old Russia was socially, politically, morally, deficient in many ways? To be sure, there were remarkable achievements, say, in economic development prior to the 1917 Revolution; but surely this is not the yardstick by which he would wish Soviet accomplishments measured. Whether he likes it or not, there were good reasons why, by the time the Provisional Government (not the Bolsheviks) replaced the Tsar's rule in 1917, the *ancien régime* had lost virtually all support in all social strata. Mr. Solzhenitsyn's own intellectual forerunners were the outstanding Russian emigré intellectuals of the nineteenth century about whom he keeps remarkably silent—the Herzens and Turgenevs and the Plekhanovs, who could not freely write and work in the Russia of their day either.

Aleksandr Solzhenitsyn makes a passionate and elaborate appeal to differentiate between Russia and the Soviet Union, between the people and communism, which (as he put it elsewhere) was after all a "dark un-Russian whirlwind that descended on us from the West." Damning the West both in its bourgeois and its Marxist versions, for its lack of ethical values, much as did the Russian Slavophiles of a century ago, he would turn his back on it to keep (or make) his mythical Russia pure.

As Robert C. Tucker explained in his contribution to this exchange, it is ludicrous to deny that there were *some* things in the Russian soil—be they products of heredity or of environment—that were receptive to the peculiar adaptation of Marxism that we call Leninism. Among Americans dealing with Soviet affairs, I personally probably place less weight on traditional Russian elements in bolshevism and Soviet conduct than do most of my colleagues, but I cannot write them off and ignore them. Whether or not one accepts all of the elements in Professor Tucker's analysis, it is either naïve or disingenuous to deny that Soviet policy too has in varying proportions been a blend of distinctly communist elements and Russian national aims and impulses. Of course many Americans fail to remember that "Russian" is not the same as "Soviet" (a distinction which not all Soviet citizens observe either), but the distinction must not be absolutized: Mr. Solzhenitsyn cannot rewrite history to undo Leninism's Russian roots, nor can he deny the recent growth of Russian national self-consciousness in the U.S.S.R.

No less troublesome are his attempts to argue that, by becoming communist, people everywhere "turn their back[s] on [their] own nationality" and "embrace inhumanity." One third of the Italian electorate freely chooses to vote communist; is he suggesting that they thereby cease to be Italian? Millions followed the Chinese communists to power; does he mean to argue that they stopped being Chinese? Today the sixteen million party members in the U.S.S.R. comprise more than half of all urban males between the ages of twenty-five and fifty with a college education; are these no longer Russians, Uzbeks, Ukrainians, Georgians or whatever their nationality happens to be?

To be sure, it is troublesome to witness the "appeals of communism" around the world. At least for short periods, communist movements have included both some of the best and some of the worst specimens of mankind in many lands. But, whether people join or support communist parties out of ideological commitment, or for personal reasons, purposes of practical politics, or as a "union card," we cannot blithely deny them either their humanity or their nationality. Mr. Solzhenitsyn has known too many decent former communists for him to do so either. In fact, in a number of instances communism has served as an instrument for the advancement of national movements or interests.

Nor, finally, can it be seriously questioned that the Russians constitute the ruling nationality of the Soviet Union. I am not one of those who see the nationality problem as the Achilles' heel of the Soviet system (as some prominent Nazis did and as some American analysts do today). Mr. Solzhenitsyn correctly points to such nonsense as the quixotic defense of nonexistent ethnic entities like Idel-Ural and Cossackia. And to be sure, some of the non-Russian republics of the Soviet Union have benefited from more rapid economic development, precisely because they started out so far behind. But by all measures, political and military rule in the Soviet Union remains overwhelmingly in Russian hands; it is the Russian language and culture that members of other nationalities must master if they hope to move ahead; non-Russians face all the problems Russians face, plus the special problems of being non-Russians too.

Mr. Solzhenitsyn has repeatedly asserted that in its essence the Soviet system has been monolithic and unchanging; that there are no "good" or "bad" communists but that they are all alike; that there are no distinctions between Leninism and Stalinism but only one communism. This is a question of considerable importance for American policy. It is impossible to make a systematic exposition here of what any college student studying the Soviet Union learns—how Stalin's rule differed from the Lenin era; the many ways in which the Khrushchev era differed from the Stalin years that preceded it—the most obvious differences being the absence of a one-man dictator à la Stalin and the end of mass political terror which resulted in the release of Mr. Solzhenitsyn (along with millions of others) from the Gulag.

Regrettably, Mr. Solzhenitsyn accepts the Soviet argument, made in the Stalin era, that Stalin was "the Lenin of today." Stalin was one among a number of possible successors to Lenin—politically and ideologically perhaps as legitimate as the others but surely no more so. The point is that it *did* make a significant difference who wound up on top. Compared to

Trotsky and Bukharin or all other serious contenders, Stalin was unquestionably the worst. Similarly it *did* make a difference that Nikita Khrushchev emerged as the leader in the late 1950s: erratic and impulsive, he was nonetheless a greater force for change and for a more open Soviet society than his rivals and challengers, from Molotov to Suslov, would have been.

As studies of Soviet politics have shown, the Soviet regime is not immune to internal dispute—be it factionalism among members of the Politburo and Party Secretariat over issues of power, personalities, and policies; or the equivalent of interest groups seeking special advantages and policy decisions congruent with their preferences; or rivalries among different geographic and functional constituencies; or finally disputes over détente, resource allocation, the need for foreign technology, energy policy, arms control, or "socialist legality." Such disputes were more overt in the Khrushchev era than before or after, but they continue and are probably endemic in any complex system in the contemporary world. Of course these men are not democrats. (Neither is Mr. Solzhenitsyn.) What is important is the fact that, in a number of instances, it makes an enormous difference what person, what faction, or what orientation winds up in power—both for the peace of the world and for the welfare of the Soviet population. Rather than dismiss all this in advance as insignificant, as Mr. Solzhenitsyn does, we need to study more systematically and more skillfully such differences in outlook and values within the Soviet establishment, among Soviet experts and consultants, and in the Soviet public at large, and the ways in which under Soviet conditions such attitudes are shaped, aggregated, and expressed.

It would be naïve to assert that all citizens of the U.S.S.R. are firmly dedicated to the Soviet regime. It is no less simplistic to assert that "the oppressed peoples are allies of the West." If on the one hand the Soviet leaders cannot any longer be simply "immeasurably indifferent to . . . the Russian people whom they have exploited to the point of total exhaustion and near-extinction" (as our author asserts with characteristic hyperbole), they have on the other hand secured the basic acquiescence and support of at least significant parts of the population who share in their country's pride over its achievements, be it by cosmonauts or in chess; many have been effectively socialized into believing what they are taught; others have had opportunities for training and advancement for which they are grateful to the system.

Our author is profoundly mistaken if he sees the Soviet Union, China, or Cuba as the reification of "communism." If there is a threat facing the United States from the communist world, it is Soviet military force (and this is not the place to discuss how serious a threat it is), not communist ideas or beliefs. In any case, the attraction of communism as an ideology inspiring and motivating men and women has been receding; what has been growing is Soviet power. The evolution of the Sino-Soviet dispute from arguments primarily ideological in nature, a generation ago, to a conflict of rival nation-states today, is a good example in point.

No less important, the role of communist elements in the world view and motivation of Soviet (and other communist) leaders has changed importantly over time. These are admittedly difficult matters to probe, if only because of the frantic insistence of Soviet spokesmen that they never depart from the canons of orthodoxy. What is more, and I am embarrassed to state such self-evident observations, the formal commitment to a body of doctrine tells us nothing about its role in motivating (rather than justifying) behavior or in shaping perceptions. Marx and Lenin had mighty little to say about matters on which the men in the Kremlin must make decisions, day in and day out—ICBMs, garbage disposal, cloning, or computer hardware. Those men are increasingly dependent on the advice of specialists whose competence, in science and technology or in world affairs, appears to be on the increase (some high Soviet officials consider such reliance dangerous in itself, but that only adds another dimension to the internal dialogue which Mr. Solzhenitsyn does not wish to recognize).

Mr. Solzhenitsyn's familiarity with the American scene is limited at best, as some of his earlier speeches and writings have made clear. It is understandable therefore that he cannot make a fair judgment of American scholarship on the Soviet Union or of foreign policy attitudes toward the U.S.S.R. His arbitrary selection of specimens amounts to little more than a caricature of American writing. He ignores both the valuable work that has been done and the wide diversity of views, many of which he lumps together in his polemic.

Most deplorable perhaps are the pot shots which he contemptuously takes across the entire landscape of American public and academic life. He has—it pains me to say—a lot to learn about the morals of public denunciation in our society. I yield to no one in my fundamental disagreement with the political views of Richard Pipes. But I will defend him as an honest and dedicated scholar, well informed in the areas of his genuine expertise. Perhaps Mr. Solzhenitsyn has unwittingly absorbed more of the political culture of his native milieu than he is aware of if he insists on maligning those he disagrees with in such a familiar "amalgam" of charges.

His essay argues, as earlier ones have, that we are on the eve of a global battle between good and evil, between "world humanity" and "world communism" (never mind that the latter has irreversibly fallen apart). "To coexist with communism on the same planet is impossible," he asserts.

Such a passionate ideological perspective is a poor counsel for an intelligent American foreign policy. From Woodrow Wilson to Jimmy Carter our experience with the pursuit of ideological objectives abroad has been little short of disastrous. Mr. Solzhenitsyn's single-minded belief in the efficacy of armed force in combating the Soviet Union reinforces the unfortunate proclivity in American politics to rely on brute military force as a substitute for political expertise and for the use of diplomacy, trade, or cultural affairs to cultivate Soviet-American relations.

"Simplicity," Henry Adams once wrote, "is the most deceitful mistress that ever betrayed man." Soviet reality is so much more complex, the trends in Soviet policy and society are so much more varied, ambiguous, and open-ended than his dialectic allows, that his approach to both Soviet and American problems must be deemed seriously misleading.

This is not the place to examine the depth of Mr. Solzhenitsyn's political values. No one will wish to challenge his right to develop and propound them. He stands in a long tradition of Russian writers, such as Leo Tolstoy and Fyodor Dostoyevsky, who similarly liked to evolve idiosyncratic political and philosophical ideas. It remains to hope that, like those other great Russian writers, Aleksandr Solzhenitsyn will be remembered first and foremost for his marvelous works of fiction, as well as his books resting on personal experience.

ALEXANDER DALLIN
Professor of History and
Political Science
Stanford University

Palo Alto, California
Fall 1980

Mr. Solzhenitsyn replied as follows:

THE COURAGE TO SEE

Involvement in political polemics exposes one to a chorus of hackneyed accusations: I am said to idealize the Russian past, to be ignorant of the history of my own country, and of course to lack all understanding of America and the modern world (no doubt because I spend little of my time chatting at filling stations). In my essay I cautioned against malicious distortions of Russian history; this is now being represented as my complete system of views. The history of the Russian Revolution has been the object of my research for over forty years now, and I am presently completing an account in eight volumes which will begin appearing in Russian in 1982 and perhaps three years later in English. A large-scale literary analysis of this sort reveals flaws and errors in the development of Russia over the ages that are far more substantial than anything my ardent opponents can point out to me from superficial newspaper reports and the latest fads and fashions. While political polemics, which inevitably coarsen the issues, are no place for the writer, it is painful to hear flimsy and irresponsible judgments pronounced with a scholarly air, even while witnessing the West's astonishing helplessness and lack of resourcefulness in the current world situation, especially in the realm of ideas and in the caliber of those entrusted with their execution. Under such circumstances, it is difficult to delay speaking out for another five years.

I

A good indicator of the viability of any system is its receptiveness to criticism. I had always assumed that the American system desires criticism and even appreciates it. This belief was shaken after my Harvard address, when amid the torrents of journalistic fury there was no mistaking the cries of "mind your own business," "shut up," and even "get out." It was a surprise, frankly, to hear the same notes sounded in the pages of *Foreign Affairs* (Silvio J. Treves). I had no intention of "lecturing" anyone; I wished to share the experience of living under communist rule. Nothing could be simpler for me than to keep my peace and leave the concern for America's future to Mr. Treves and those who share his views. Once they have experienced it all on their own backs, we shall understand each other perfectly. Yet it remains true that fear of criticism and fresh ideas is the mark of a doomed system.

Robert W. Thurston's response reads as if it had been written with the express intent of illustrating my point about how easy it is to fool a Western visitor to the U.S.S.R. With unconscious humor, he cites his ten months of personal experience —ten months of living as a foreigner under surveillance in the Soviet capital, in expertly staged showcase conditions—an experience which he intrepidly juxtaposes to the fifty-year experience of a native Soviet subject in the forbidden depths of the country. Hence the result: Mr. Thurston's discovery of "Soviet patriotism" and of "a widespread pride in the material progress the Soviet Union has made" (in metallurgy? in military production?), when in fact there is not enough to eat, sounds like an insulting quotation from *Pravda* or *The People's Daily*. A dispute about the various juridical details bearing on pre-revolutionary Russia (which, incidentally, Mr. Thurston distorts) would be out of place on the pages of *Foreign Affairs* or in the present discussion. But one marvels at his rashness in basing his conclusions about the "socialist sympathies" of Russia on the "elections" for the Constituent Assembly, elections which were held after the Bolshevik coup, when non-socialist parties were harshly restricted in their activities. The American concept of what constitutes an election has here been mechanically transferred to the peasant Russia of 1917, which did not even grasp the processes involved and which was as yet incapable of making any conscious and deliberate use of its vote. (In 1945 Americans asked Soviet citizens, "If you dislike Stalin so much, why don't you vote him out of office?")

One feels more awkward when a Sovietologist of Professor Dallin's stature assures us that half a century of first-hand observation in the areas of the Soviet Union inaccessible to foreigners is less important than "reliable insights into the motives and functioning of Soviet policymakers." To achieve such insights, it seems, one need only meet with these people and study *Pravda* closely. Yet Mr. Dallin admits elsewhere in his essay that Soviet officials *conceal* their motives. The results of such meetings are evident enough in the long succession of Western failures. Has Professor Dallin ever set eyes on the subject of his research—the expanses of this enslaved country and the inhabitants of its provincial and rural areas? Upon what data does he base his confident assertion that the Russian village is not becoming impoverished and that "the Soviet standard of living has gone up"? His pronouncements about the moon would have been more accurate, for at least the reports of the astronauts are more reliable. With reference to the Soviet provinces, where potatoes run out before spring and other foodstuffs are entirely unavailable (just because Mr. Dallin finds this hard to imagine does not make it "hyperbole"), my opponent writes in all seriousness about widespread pride in the achievements of cosmonauts and chess players. Or else he consoles us with the supposed flourishing of "politically 'safe' forms of culture." What does this mean? The humanities are shot through with lies, the exact sciences are placed in the service of the military, so what kind of "culture" does this leave? (As for the provinces, they lack even this.)

Mr. Dallin legitimately inquires about how the figures on the victims of the regime were arrived at, given the secrecy of Soviet statistics. But the calculations of Ivan Kurganov, a professor of statistics, were published in the United States sixteen years ago (*Novoye Russkoye Slovo,* April 12, 1964) in a language accessible to Professor Dallin, and it is strange that he is not aware of them. A new attempt to calculate our losses, by the recently arrested Iosif Dyadkin, was reported in *The Wall Street Journal* of July 23, 1980. One might also mention the figures compiled by Maksudov in *Cahiers du monde russe et soviètique,* Vol. 18, No. 3, July–September 1977. The totals arrived at by all these various calculations are of the same order of magnitude—tens of millions of victims. It will of course be a long time before we possess precise data: the Soviet maw does not yield up its secrets, even in confidential meetings with Soviet policymakers.

Eugen Loebl advises us to abandon excursions in to the history of communism in the U.S.S.R. and to focus our attention upon the threat that confronts us today. And yet it is true of every field of knowledge that a phenomenon can be properly understood only through an awareness of the history of its development. A great deal depends on whether one perceives communism today (including the Cuban, Vietnamese, and Chinese varieties) as a phenomenon that has a predominantly Russian pedigree or, on the other hand, as an international or even metaphysical entity: each view will call forth a different response, be it disastrous capitulation (familiar since Franklin D. Roosevelt's day) or an attempt to stand firm. Mr. Loebl's contention that communism is national in essence, just like national socialism, is entirely unpersuasive; Nazism always manifested itself in national forms and never laid claim to internationalism; it coined the concept of the *Herrenvolk* and did not lay waste its "own" nation with fire and sword, as communism has hastened to do wherever it has come to power. And it was precisely this trait which led Nazism to declare openly (in a way which communism is too devious ever to do) its intention of turning the inhabitants of the U.S.S.R. into slaves—a fact which, as Mr. Loebl correctly notes, led to its downfall. However, the author is imposing his own views upon my essay when he would have me say that only Ukrainians and Balts were ready to support Hitler. In fact I testified that all the occupied Russian lands also expected the war to bring liberation, and that this was the reason why the Red Army fled with such alacrity. But Hitler had declared war upon the Russian people as such, leaving them no way out.

And it is this same advice that is repeatedly offered to the contemporary West by those who regard the threat now looming over the world as Russian, rather than communist. Such counsel can only have the same devastating outcome.

In totalitarian states the restoration of historical truth is viewed as the most subversive of activities, one that merits persecution of the harshest type. But even in the West truth cannot be established as long as careless and uninformed statements are tolerated. To quote Mr. Loebl, Russia was "the most reactionary government at the end of the century and the ally of all oppressive governments." One wonders what governments Mr. Loebl could have in mind? In point of fact, at the end of the nineteenth century (from 1892 on) Russia had only one ally—republican France. In 1907, in addition, Russia became formally allied to England. Mr. Loebl writes that, "the tsarist dream of world domination caught the soul of the Russian nation." But in the nineteenth century the only "Tsar" who nurtured dreams of world conquest was Napoleon. Nowhere else were these aspirations to be found, except perhaps in the vast British Empire sprawling over five continents. Can Mr. Loebl point to anything in Russian literature, art, or folklore that might suggest a thirst for world domination? Or did he use some other method to detect this desire in the "soul of the Russian nation"? "Russian culture . . . is the preferred one all over the Soviet Union," writes Mr. Loebl. He can be forgiven for not knowing what constitutes Russian culture, but he should not pass judgment on the basis of journalistic hearsay. I can attest that *Russian* culture was crushed and destroyed with a vengeance in the very first decade of Soviet rule. What we are seeing today is an atheistic and anti-national *Soviet culture* masquerading as "Russian culture"—and moreover doing so in a sullied and bastardized form of the Russian language. The interests of communist Moscow are "first of all Russian interests," claims Mr. Loebl, who has evidently skipped entire sections of my essay, where

I point out that no nationality under Soviet rule has been ravaged to the extent that the Russians have.

Mr. Loebl is not an exception and one can come upon instances of similarly irresponsible statements among still more prominent Americans. Thus Professor Stephen F. Cohen, Director of Russian Studies at Princeton University, writes in *The New Republic* of December 29, 1979: "During the first and second five-year plans [i.e., 1928–1937] . . . a mostly backward . . . society was transformed into a predominantly industrial one . . . with many of the benefits of a modern welfare state." A fantastic statement! Were it known in my country, it would be read as sheer mockery: these words are applied to a decade which saw wholesale destitution, hunger, bread rationing in peacetime, six million deaths from starvation in the Ukraine alone, the extermination of 15 million sturdy peasants, the end of agricultural abundance, an abrupt halt to the production of consumer goods, acute shortages of clothing, footwear, and household goods throughout the land—and all this in the name of heavy industry and showplace stores for foreigners in Moscow. During this era of atavistic privation and brutality, which Professor Cohen likens to a "modern welfare state," the last prewar year of 1913 seemed like a long-lost miracle to the population of my country. And in the past seventy years our country has never so much as approached the abundance of that "tsarist" year.

When the Director of Russian Studies at a leading university commits such a blunder one cannot really be surprised to hear one of the American presidential candidates, Edward Kennedy, declare that meat shortages are no threat to the Soviet leadership: they would "simply" feed the population chicken instead. Here is a man who aspires to direct the politics and economics of the world, yet has no inkling of the simple but telling fact that chicken is worth its weight in gold in the U.S.S.R., and is not even available to patients on special diets.

This comfortable bed of illusions, this seemingly deliberate self-deception, is a characteristic trait shared by the Western press and many Western politicians; wishful thinking is sustained by verbal incantation. For example, in June 1945, *The New York Times* lent its authority (why?) to the allegation that the Katyn murders were committed by the Nazis, rather than by the communists. This urge to deal in illusions rather than in facts, which has since become almost universal, together with the ready acceptance of unscrupulous fables about Russian and Soviet history, serves to blind the West in this time of danger, preventing it from grasping its true predicament and from finding a way out. It is as if the West actually does not *want* to know the truth until the moment when this knowledge has ceased to be of use.

II

It is clear that Robert C. Tucker's essay reflects not only his personal opinions but the established views of a milieu which exerts a formative influence upon U.S. policy: whether Democrats or Republicans are in power, and regardless of who is in the White House, the leading experts and advisers are drawn from these same circles. (It is symptomatic that Professor Dallin concurs with the essential arguments of Professor Tucker.)

At the core of the problem lies a misunderstanding of the nature of communism: a failure to acknowledge it as the quintessence of dynamic and implacable evil (of course "evil" today is considered an unscientific concept, almost a four-letter word, for instead of "good" and "evil" there exists only a multiplicity of opinions, each one as valid as the next), a failure to recognize it as an international and universal historical phenomenon (an extreme manifestation of socialism), rather than a local Russian episode. And this leads to a wider misunderstanding of contemporary Soviet reality.

Anyone who takes the time to read Mr. Tucker's letter

carefully will discern the author's sympathy for a "pure" communism, for its early Leninist phase, as well as the absence of any condemnation of Marxist doctrine. Mr. Tucker might well be reluctant to express this today in so many words, but it is apparent in the very structure of his thought. That is why he is obliged to shift all the evils of communism onto the Stalin years and thence to probe back into the Russian sixteenth and fifteenth centuries in his search for origins. Mr. Tucker doubts whether the Lenin period had a Gulag system, denies that forced labor as such existed in Lenin's concentration camps, and even seems to justify these camps on the grounds that they were set up only "to imprison opponents of the Bolshevik regime," while in reality anyone who stood out from the crowd would end up in the camps alongside all those whose behavior or social origins happened to displease the Bolsheviks. (This is all set forth at sufficient length in *The Gulag Archipelago,* and I invite Professor Tucker to undertake a task which the Soviet regime has not so far ventured to tackle: to refute my book point by point.)

The time has come to call a spade a spade: it is time to admit that the October coup masterminded by Lenin and Trotsky against the weak Russian democracy was an act of villainy; that it was carried out with significant financial aid from Wilhelm's Germany; that the communism of the early years was a system every bit as sordid, devious, cruel and inhuman as was communism under Stalin; that credit for inventing the Gulag system of forced labor with its multi-million convict population belongs to Trotsky (his forced "labor armies"); that Trotsky is likewise the immoral inventor of an early version of the "gas chamber"—barges scuttled at sea with hundreds of prisoners aboard; that he too is responsible for the mass execution of draftees who refused to fight for the Bolsheviks; that the genocide on the Don, the slaughter of 1.2 million Cossack civilians, was launched by the same two luminaries. The idea of granting the peasants land as a propaganda gesture, then promptly reclaiming it, harvest and all, belongs to Lenin. It was he who declared war on the well-to-do peasants (whose prosperity was actually less than that of an average American farmer), with the thousands of executions this entailed. It was Lenin who drove peasants into tightly regulated communes and artels, Lenin who suppressed every non-communist publication, and Lenin, together with Trotsky, who smashed the labor unions and the independent workers' movement (the so-called Congresses of Factory Representatives). It is inordinately euphemistic to refer to this regime as "authoritarian," as Mr. Tucker does—yet he seems unable to bring himself to pronounce the word "totalitarian" with respect to it.

Reading through the correspondence of Marx and Engels, the most complete edition of which has been published in Russian (and hence is accessible to Professor Tucker), we might well be staggered by the two conspirators' total lack of principles and scruples and their "fierce insistence on orthodoxy" (a Russian trait, Mr. Tucker assures us), were we not already familiar with innumerable later examples from communist states around the world. In the formulations of Marx and Engels we can readily identify both their ferocious atheism (the philosophical core of their system), and their equally ferocious intolerance and hatred of every rival faction within the party. This vehement hatred was, upon occasion, even directed against entire Slavic peoples. Here are some samples of their more celebrated pronouncements:

"There is only one way of shortening, simplifying, and concentrating the bloodthirsty death-throes of the old society and the bloody birth pangs of the new—revolutionary terror." (Marx and Engels, *Sochineniia* [*Works*], Second Edition, Moscow: Gospolitizdat, 1955–77, Vol. 5, p. 494.)

"We are pitiless and we ask for no pity from you. When our time comes, we shall not conceal terrorism with hypocritical phrases." (*Ibid.,* Vol. 6, p. 548.)

"The vengeance of the people will break forth with such ferocity that not even the year 1793 enables us to envisage it." (*Ibid.*, Vol. 2, p. 515.)

"[Workers must] counteract the efforts of the bourgeoisie to restore calm, and force the democrats to implement their current terroristic statements. . . . Not only [should they] not oppose so-called excesses, those popular acts of vengeance directed at hated individuals or official buildings . . . but [they should] take the lead in these matters." (*Ibid.*, Vol. 7, p. 263.)

"Coercion (i.e., state power) is also an economic force." (*Ibid.*, Vol. 37, p. 420.)

"Political freedom . . . is worse than the most abject slavery." (*Sochineniia,* First Edition, Moscow-Leningrad: Marx-Engels-Lenin Institute, 1928–48, Vol. 2, p. 394.)

"Looking into the future, I can discern something that will strongly smack of high treason; this seems as inevitable as fate itself." (*Ibid.*, Vol. 22, p. 138.)

". . . thanks to the perplexity and flabbiness of all the others, our party will be forced into government one fine morning . . . we shall be constrained to undertake communist experiments and extravagant measures, the untimeliness of which we know better than anyone else . . . until the world is able to form a historical judgment of such events, we shall be considered . . . 'beasts,' which doesn't matter!" (*Ibid.*, Vol. 25, p. 187.)

Marx and Engels reiterated on many occasions that "once we are at the helm, we shall be obliged to reenact the year 1793."

Lenin, too, was not one to conceal his historical origins, nor did he ascribe them to Russian traditions. He constantly cited Marx and Engels, swore by their names, and applied their theories in practice (which does not make communism a German phenomenon). He also followed them in expressing unabashed admiration for Jacobin terror—both for the wholesale executions and mass drownings of condemned prisoners. He used to say that "terror renews a country," and made no secret of the fact that he was following Babeuf's injunction that the conquered classes must be completely destroyed. (But neither does this make communism French.) It was during the time of the French Revolution that violence came to be meted out according to class allegiance. Both in name and structure the "revolutionary tribunals" and even the "extraordinary commissions" (known as "Cheka" in Soviet times from the Russian abbreviation of this phrase) are based on Jacobin models and have nothing to do with Ivan the Terrible or the sixteenth century. The similarities between Bolsheviks and Jacobins in both theory and tactics are utterly obvious to anyone who takes the trouble to study the historical evidence. (This is true down to the smallest details: the prohibition of a free press; the crushing of rival factions; the proclamation of dictatorship as "the highest form of freedom"; monolithic unity of the entire population; the merging of the state with the party, with the latter dictatorially controlled by a single individual; even food requisitioning detachments sent out to rob the peasants, the physical destruction of churches, the melting down of church bells, and the confiscation of church valuables.)

Curiously, Professor Tucker seems never to have heard of any of this or else has never given any thought to these direct and obvious continuities. In what purports to be a scholarly exposition, he adduces a remarkably frivolous argument in support of the "profoundly Russian" origins of bolshevism, namely that Berdyaev thought so!

Has not mere invocation of other authorities long ceased to serve as a substitute for reasoned argument in any branch of scholarship? I venture to note, furthermore, that there was something decidedly whimsical about Berdyaev's philosophical views. At least twice, and arguably three times in the course of his career, Berdyaev underwent a 180-degree change in perspective, in each case attacking his former views as something completely alien to himself.[1] His book on communism in Russia does not amount to an objective historical study or an analysis of historical data; instead it is a manifestation of his personal and inconstant philosophical tendencies, which culminated in his decision to fly the red Soviet flag from his house. Many processes familiar the world over he implausibly ascribes to Russia alone, such as the substitution of social forms of activity for religious ones. He even goes so far as to call the inhuman teachings of Marxism an "ethical doctrine," and to declare that Marx and Lenin "wished to do good"—words which resound like blasphemy over the corpses of tormented millions and before the brutal visage of today's world-conquering power. Berdyaev concedes that Russian history has experienced "interruptions in its organic evolution"—yet simultaneously, and in complete contradiction, bases his whole argument on an "organic tradition," which he derives at will either from Muscovite Russia or from its virtual antithesis, St. Petersburg Russia, whichever seems more convenient.

Berdyaev, however, was writing in 1937, when the phenomenon of communism had yet to emerge in its full historical dimensions. But how can anyone still maintain in 1980—when communist regimes control twenty-five countries, span four continents and represent every race on earth—that communism, including its far-flung International of Terror in some twenty other countries, is shaped by peculiarly Russian features?

Mr. Tucker's notion that the Stalinist phase of the communist leviathan was created by drawing on the sixteenth and eighteenth centuries of Russian history is not merely unscholarly, but has an impressionistic, fantastic ring. How can one seriously argue that Stalin needed the example of Ivan the

---

[1] See for example, N. Poltoratzky, *Berdiaev i Rossia: Filosofiia istorii Rossii u N.A. Berdiaeva* (Berdyaev and Russia: N.A. Berdyaev's Philosophy of the History of Russia), New York, 1967, in Russian.

Terrible before he could lop off the heads of his foes and strike terror in the hearts of his subjects? Does this mean that but for Ivan the Terrible he would never have hit on the idea? Are tyrannies so few and far between in the history of the world? The great profundity that a tyrant should keep his people in fear and trembling Stalin could have picked up from any primer in world history, or from the history of feudal Georgia, or even before that from the recesses of his own cunning and malevolent heart. For whatever else we may say, this much at least he could grasp intuitively from the outset, and without recourse to books. Or again, Mr. Tucker traces the origins of the Gulag system back to the practice of forced labor under the Peter the Great. It would thus seem that forced labor was a Russian invention! But why not cite the pharaohs of Egypt, or closer in time, the democracies of England, France and Holland, all of which employed forced labor in their colonies, while the United States made use of it even on in its own soil —in each case after Peter's time. And what schoolboy has not read about galley slaves? (The point of Professor Tucker's quotation from George Kennan is altogether obscure, unless he wished to demonstrate that foreign observers were granted access to the hard labor prison system [*katorga*] in pre-revolutionary Russia, no less than they were to the law courts. It would not be difficult to find more vivid descriptions of hard labor in New Caledonia in French literature, but what does that prove about the Fifth Republic?)[2] Territorial aggrandizement is likewise proclaimed a primordial Russian trait, even though England had seized a good deal more terri-

[2]When the translation of Dostoyevsky's *Notes from the House of the Dead* was first published in England (in 1881), a review in one of the leading British journals noted that Dostoyevsky's description points to laxities and indulgences in the Russian treatment of convicts "the idea of which would horrify an English warder" (*The Athenaeum*, No. 2788, April 2, 1881, p. 455). The considerably greater privations of British convicts were also noted in *The Academy* (Vol. 19, No. 467, April 16, 1881, p. 273).

tory and France did not lag far behind. Are we to conclude from this that the English and the French are inherently predatory peoples? And last but not least the collective farm, that embodiment of the universal socialist principle of the commune, is interpreted by Mr. Tucker as a manifestation of Russian serfdom.

Is it scholarly procedure to announce as a fact the transfer of various governmental and institutional features across four centuries of history in the absence of any transmitting or transferring agents, be they parties, classes, or individuals, and with casual disregard for the obliteration of all social institutions in 1917? This must clearly have been some kind of mystical transference, evidently via the genes. (Or, to adopt Professor Dallin's more elegant formulation: there were *"some* things in the Russian soil—be they products of heredity or of environment" that must have been receptive to Marxism.) And what curious scholarship leads Mr. Tucker simultaneously "not to notice" the direct and obvious line of succession whereby each of the essential traditions and institutions of the Stalin era was inherited ready-made from across an interval of a mere five to ten years—inherited from Lenin and Trotsky: the same Cheka- GPU-NKVD, these same troikas (or "special boards") in lieu of trials (why bring in Alexander III?), the same Gulag (already in existence), the same Article 58, the same mass terror, the same party, the same ideology—and all this within the same generation and through the agency of the same individuals (who had an opportunity to murder in both periods), and the same principle of intensive industrialization put forward by Trotsky, whereby the needs of the people are suppressed and all is cast into the voracious maw of heavy industry. (The "ambiguities" in the legacies of Lenin and Trotsky which Mr. Dallin seeks are simply not there to be found.)

I refuse to believe that Professor Tucker could be so utterly blind to all these facts. I can only regard this as a conscious effort to whitewash the early communist regime, to pass over its iniquitous crimes and institutions as if they never existed but were invented later by Stalin (the alleged "destroyer" of bolshevism), in emulation of the Russian tradition. What "revolution from above" (the threadbare Marxist term adopted by Mr. Tucker) is Stalin supposed to have carried out? He consolidated the Leninist legacy dutifully and consistently within the forms in which he had inherited it. But even if Mr. Tucker (and the many who share his views) were able to achieve the impossible and to prove that the Cheka, the revolutionary tribunals, the systematic use of hostages, the robbing of the people, the rigidly enforced uniformity of opinion, the party ideology and dictatorship, were all inspired not by fellow communists and not by the Jacobins, but by Ivan the Terrible and Peter the Great—even then Mr. Tucker's theory of a "Russian tradition" would miss the mark. For in fact nationally minded Russian thinkers have long regarded both of these Tsars as objects not of adulation but of censure, while in the popular awareness and in folklore the first of them has been damned as a villain and the second as an "anti-Christ." The fact that Peter did much to *destroy* the Russian way of life, its customs, consciousness and national character, and to suppress religion (in the teeth of popular revolt) is too obvious and familiar a point to dwell on.

Worldwide communist subversion, the practice of economic sabotage, terrorism, insurrection, and ideological warfare—can all this represent a primordial Russian tradition? The explosive situation in central Asia today clearly illustrates the difference. It is true that Russia seized the emirate of Bukhara (not Afghanistan) during the nineteenth century, at a time when the democratic states of Europe also felt no moral qualms about waging wars of conquest (England, too, tried to take Afghanistan, but failed). I acknowledge with sorrow and shame that my country participated along with the rest of Europe in the subjugation of weaker nations, but the fifty years of the Russian protectorate in Central Asia were at a time of peace: religion, customs and personal liberty were not suppressed, and there was not so much as a movement for revolt. Lenin, by contrast, had scarcely seized power when he began preparing, in 1921, to lay hands on Turkey, Persia and Afghanistan under the pretext of a "revolutionary federation." By 1922, the methods used by the communists in the Khiva and Bukhara regions provoked a Muslim insurrection similar to that in Afghanistan today. It raged for ten years into the period of Stalin's rule when it was finally crushed by unprecedented reprisals against the population. That is the "tradition" to which the invasion of Afghanistan belongs.

I am well aware that the term "Stalinism" (as both Mr. Tucker and Mr. Dallin point out) was coined in the 1920s by the Trotskyite faction in its struggle with Stalin. But its present-day usage—to describe a fully developed twenty-five-year period in the evolution of a vast communist state—is a diversionary tactic calculated to mask the irreconcilably anti-human essence of communism, the main threat to the world today.

Does the fact that communism is an international phenomenon rule out the possibility of any national peculiarities or local variants? Not really, since communism has to operate in a real world, among an actual people, and must, like it or not, avail itself of that nation's language, (albeit mutilating it to suit its own purposes). Thus, in China wall posters are suppressed and in the U.S.S.R.—*samizdat.* Russian city dwellers are herded out to gather potatoes and Cubans to harvest sugar cane. In the Soviet Union people were exterminated by exile to the tundra, in Cambodia they were driven into the jungle. Yugoslavia adopted its own set of tactics: after hastily getting his mass murders out of the way in 1945, Tito turned meek as a lamb in order to obtain Western aid. And Ceausescu adroitly secured a measure of independence in foreign affairs, but only at the cost of a massive intensification of the totalitarian climate within his country. East German communism would have it that there is no need for national reunification. North Korean communism claims the opposite. (I am not sure what gave Mr. Dallin the idea that I regard every Italian who votes communist and every Uzbek who joins the Party under pressure as having surrendered his nationality. What I said was that nationality is suppressed by the communist *system* and is forfeited by the leaders and zealots of that system. There was thus no real need for Mr. Dallin to make this logical error. "In a number of instances," Mr. Dallin assures us, "communism has served as an instrument for the advancement of national movements or interests," and this is indeed a view once held in the United States with respect to North Vietnam. Of late, however, such confidence appears to have been dispelled. Is it not now obvious to one and all that neither in Estonia nor Poland nor Mongolia nor anywhere else has communism ever served national interests?)

Why not bolster communist propaganda with a clever play on national sentiment? Communist governments do so without a qualm. But does this really mean that "communism varies from country to country"? On the contrary, it is everywhere alike: everywhere totalitarian, everywhere bent on crushing individuality, conscience, even life itself, everywhere backed up by ideological terror and everywhere aggressive. The ultimate goal of world communism in all its variants is the subjugation of the entire planet, America included. One can understand why Professor Dallin should take professional offense at such a distasteful simplification of the problem. Kremlinologists would prefer to see it discussed in terms of the finer shades of ideological commitment among the communist leaders. Yet ideology commits these leaders to actions, regardless of their personal convictions, commits them in particular to an endless series of takeovers throughout the world which make no sense in terms of their personal interests: as if in a frenzy they seize Angola, then Ethiopia, then Afghanistan. It does poor service to the interests of American foreign policy to propose playing upon the "subtle variations" among the different forms of communism.

In a bid to prove me wrong, my own personal experience is trotted out as proof of the visible evolution of communism: after all, under Stalin Solzhenitsyn was in prison, under Khrushchev, *Ivan Denisovich* was published, while under Brezhnev, the man was deported. This handy motif, which has gone the rounds from one essay to the next, duly turns up in Mr. Tucker's response! Could this be because no other positive example apart from *Ivan Denisovich* has been found for the last sixty-three years? (And if *Ivan Denisovich* had never appeared, it would no doubt have been even more convenient for my critics, for they could then have argued either that there had been no camps whatever under communism, or else that the Russian people are incapable of saying anything about them on their own.) But the case of Khrushchev is precisely the exception that proves the rule: of all the communist leaders he alone was overthrown by intraparty strife for his occasional stumbling steps away from communist dogma and toward humanity; certainly none of the others in the Lenin-Trotsky-Sverdlov-Stalin-Molotov-Brezhnev succession ever strayed in this direction by so much as a foot. And even Khrushchev remained true to that fundamental and demonic tenet of Marxism: its virulent hatred of religion.

In its time communism has made use of tactical maneuvers a good bit more ambitious than *Ivan Denisovich,* such as the New Economic Policy, Stalin's hypocritical "restoration" of the concept of Church and Motherland, the "struggle for peace" during the years when America had a monopoly on nuclear arms, "letting a hundred flowers bloom," "peaceful coexistence," even the Soviet withdrawal from Austria and now "détente." What is demonstrated by all of this is not the changing nature of communism, but its flexibility and relentlessness.

It is regrettable that in taking issue with me, Mr. Tucker (and Mr. Dallin too) evades the crucial question of whether communism (in its "pure" Marxist form) is evil or whether it is not. Is it capable of becoming "kind" and healing itself? Does it threaten to crush the rest of the world in its serpentine coils or does it not?

While steering clear of this question, Mr. Tucker is quick to warn the world of an incomparably greater danger, "a most malignant form of extreme [Russian] nationalism" which is "germinating" among the vanquished, leaderless, devastated, and barely surviving Russian people.

III

The fruitfulness of any political theory may be judged by its practical results. The theory that communism is an essentially Russian phenomenon, that communism and the Russian people are indivisible and that they must be fought as a single foe, reduplicates the insane and self-defeating tactics of Hitler. But that is not the only way in which this theory fosters illusions at the expense of reality, for it would have us regard the communist Soviet Union of today as heir to the former Russia, *ergo* as a "normal" state, one which pursues its own interests and those of its citizens, a state with which we may deal along traditional lines, entering into sensible agreements, negotiations, and compromises, and apportioning spheres of influence. Yet this *could scarcely be further from the truth:* no communist government cares about the interests of its citizens or relies upon public opinion; indeed they are even ready to sacrifice their populations in the interests of international victory. (Perhaps the example of nearby Cuba is easier to recognize.) As a result, no real compromise with communism is possible; there is no way of placating, bribing, or appeasing it, and the series of concessions which the West has made serves only to weaken its own position. It is quite wrong to think that the Soviet regime is pursuing its own interests as a state: this endless aggression the world over and the outlay of capital and human life on one continent after another bring nothing but hardship to the peoples of the Soviet Union. Yet nothing, and this includes the personalities of individual rulers, can arrest communism's expansionist impulse. The very existence of other countries in the world which enjoy economic advantages or greater civil liberties is intolerable to the communist states for it confronts their populations with an enviable alternative way of life. It is imperative that such countries be conquered and crushed. Communism is simply not explicable in diplomatic, juridical or economic terms.

But communism's greatest success involves not military conquest but a propaganda victory: the rest of the world accepts that it has "mellowed" and believes in the "good" variants of communism. The Western world obligingly adopts the very *language* of communism, calling the tyrannical regimes of Eastern Europe "people's democracies," and the subversive campaign to undermine the West from within—"détente." In the early months of the communist regime in Cambodia, some Western newspapers, parroting the official line from Phnom Penh, referred to the ongoing genocide as a "peasant revolution." At the same time, the pages of leading American newspapers are open to Soviet agents who ridicule the very existence of Soviet aggression and deceitfully lull Americans into the belief that communism is not an international movement and thus threatens no one. Conversely, it seems inconceivable to the Western reading public that malnutrition is rife in the Soviet Union and China today, that the population lacks basic commodities, and that food rationing is commonplace. In fact, this is dismissed as "anti-communist propaganda." A real war has been going on for thirty-five years, there has been a long string of Western retreats and the loss of more than twenty countries, and yet the West persists in referring to this Third World War as "peaceful coexistence." Presidents have come and gone and with them their Secretaries of State and their advisers in the White House and State Department, but the same old thinking persists and there are no new ideas: we see the same precarious balancing act based on ever more "subtle distinctions" between various brands of communism, factions and their leaders—which in reality means concessions and capitulations, each one dragging the West steadily deeper into the abyss. (The next batch of concessions may well be maturing in the State Department at this very moment.) And now we hear the clamoring of an idea that does claim to be new: instead of warning us against the mighty juggernaut that has already crushd one-half of mankind and is set to destroy the remainder, they would have us fear a rebirth of a nationally conscious Russia, a renascence which can only be salutary.

There are no new ideas, and it would be strange were any to arise amid the smug secularism which cannot see beyond itself.

In matters more important than the sale of a particular batch of goods, the theory of "subtle distinctions" between various types of communism (or, as Mr. Dallin puts it, "significant variations within communism," "variations, gradations, and changes," "a more differentiated and balanced understanding," and "a sophisticated approach") is not only ineffectual, but could actually prove fatal to the West. At a time when America itself is menaced by this pernicious supranational force, it is proposed that we put our faith in a sudden outburst of benevolence which will lead communism to renounce its aggressive ways, that we believe in the existence of "peace-loving Soviet leaders" (notably Brezhnev), and in the advent of a new, more mellow and amenable generation. Hopes are held out that the communist governments of Eastern Europe and Asia might suddenly withdraw their allegiance from Moscow (the West drew no significant strength from the defections of Albania and North Korea, while that of

Romania brought only hardship to its own people); to that end trading concessions are used in a bid to win these countries over (thus easing the economic burden of the U.S.S.R.). We are encouraged to expect a split in the European communist movement (the French Communist Party's dabbling in independence was fairly short-lived, and every communist party would readily volunteer the services of its personnel and organization to rule the country the moment it was occupied). We are told that the Vietnamese, Cuban, Angolan, and Ethiopian communists and other malignant offshoots of communism throughout the world will pursue their own national interests and willingly be reconciled with the United States. It is even suggested that Islam will prove the undoing of the communist movement.

Not one of these fanciful hopes has yet borne fruit except for the Sino-Soviet split, and this has now become the cornerstone of American plans and aspirations. China is already perceived as if it were not a communist country at all, as if it did not persecute its billion-strong population. But China, just like the Soviet Union in the 1930s, urgently needs technological aid from the West and is prepared to that end to don the mask of respectability. But one can be sure that in the depths of the country, hostility toward America and hatred of the American way of life are inculcated in the Chinese people just as before; the authorities could turn the nation against the United States almost overnight. And even this "moderate" China of today, as unyielding in its conduct of foreign affairs as any other communist state, is pressing the Americans to abandon their defense of Taiwan and now proposes that they withdraw from South Korea. In due course China will begin to weigh the relative advantages of confrontation or accommodation with the Soviet Union. (The dismantling of the cult of Mao that we see in China today is a step in this direction.) The failure of American diplomacy with regard to China is an all too familiar one: it consists in regarding as a "normal state" what is in reality a latent communist aggressor which is still gathering its strength.

For thirty-five years—one third of a century!—the United States and the West as a whole have chosen the path of self-induced defeat. The pattern has by now assumed historic proportions and its consequences can no longer be averted. When the United States began its withdrawal it could still boast an overwhelming military superiority, but today Washington is jolted by the discovery that the balance of world power has shifted against the West: smug complacency has allowed the scales to tilt the other way. Having given way in the past, the West finds it all the harder now to stand its ground, and harder still to make up for its losses. But the greatest weakness of all is not military but psychological. Everyone, from young men of draft age through government leaders, is banking on things turning out well in the end and shrinks from making bold and selfless decisions before it is too late and these same individuals are forced to fight in defense of their own soil. The West is morally unprepared for confrontation and strife, and will not face up to the extent of the danger, which by now may well be irreversible. The West continues to pin its hopes on a spurious "détente," which for the U.S.S.R. is the most convenient form of protracted warfare, and the one most likely to end in victory. The Soviet leaders would certainly prefer to achieve their international objectives by means of "détente," terrorism and coups d'état: why should they desire a global war, especially a nuclear one? (It is doubtful, most fortunately for mankind, that nuclear war has any real place in the strategies of the two sides: the Soviet leaders have every reason to believe that they can conquer the globe without it, while the West is morally inhibited from launching a nuclear attack except in retaliation. In any case, the "success" which the West could hope to achieve from nuclear weapons would be a hollow one, since it would be annihilating not so much its actual enemies as its potential allies, the enslaved nations.) Although this illusory "détente" enables the West to delay still further the moment of direct confrontation, this only means that the eventual clash will take place under circumstances immeasurably less to its advantage. Soon enough the United States will feel the temperature rising along its southern border; as it is, the Cuban pistol has been aimed at the soft underbelly of the American mainland for twenty years. All it needs is for the United States to increase still further its present encouragement of the Nicaraguan communists and of the Panamanian revolutionaries— a policy which has already drawn praise from that accomplished butcher Castro—and the Southern Front against the United States will be ready. For twenty years this Cuban pistol aimed with impunity at the United States has served as a daily reminder to the world of the humiliation of American principles and of America's progressive enfeeblement. American foreign policy today amounts to a series of limp and timorous maneuvers designed to placate and curry favor with potential enemies. (But it will achieve nothing in Zimbabwe, Angola or Nicaragua, and supplying nuclear technology to India with the thought of enticing it away from the U.S.S.R. will prove to be another empty hope.) Even those who favor dealing firmly with communism still cling to the illusion that communism may be pressured into undertaking internal democratic reforms. Not a chance!

Only if we acknowledge the reality of the threat to the world and the essentially international nature of communist strategy, only if we understand that the West cannot avoid a conflict with communism and cannot even postpone it for very much longer—only then will the West be capable of abandoning its squalid accommodation with oppressive regimes and undertaking a proud, principled and open defense of freedom throughout the world—from Cuba to Tibet and from the Volga to Berlin. Only an insight into the implacable essence of communism can provide guidance for a realistic course of action, one which may yet save mankind in spite of all the surrenders and squandered opportunities of the past. The crucial point is that *all* nations enslaved by communism, from the Cubans close to your shores to the Russians in the stronghold of your adversary, are victims and enemies of communism, and hence your natural allies. The West is so sensitive to the wishes of the Third World nations, yet so deaf to the aspirations of those living in communist lands. The only sound policy for the United States is to abandon its flirtations with every insurgent in every precariously neutral land, to stop trying to ingratiate itself with every Soviet emissary, the representative not of his people but of a ruling coterie, to give up its hair-splitting attempts to strike a balance between imaginary rival factions within the communist ranks—and instead to side openly with each and every enslaved nation against the universal slave driver which is communism. It is time to open a propaganda offensive as powerful and effective as that conducted against your country by the communists for sixty years, without fearing the abuse that the mendacious *Pravda* will spew out in response. In my essay I expressed astonishment at the mindless way in which the West has relinquished the mighty non-military force which resides in the air waves and whose kindling power in the midst of the communist darkness cannot even be grasped by the Western imagination. This could be the way of establishing direct contact with the subjugated peoples and of furthering the growth of their self-awareness and emancipation. (The radio and television stations of the West are, in their present form, far from ready to assume this role. The "Russian Section" of Radio Liberty, for example, despite its many years of experience, has come to be disastrously out of touch with the Russian population and with Russian interests as a result of its systematic aloofness from and even hostility to the Russian national consciousness.) All this will take a radical break with the traditions of international "etiquette," which in any case have long since been trampled by the communists, and which have shown their true worth in Tehran.

To rescue the West from the situation in which it finds itself today will require bold decisions by outstanding leaders and a rejection of routine thinking.

I might just as well not have hurried to present all these arguments. It is becoming increasingly clear that no essay of mine, nor ten such essays, nor ten individuals such as I, are capable of transmitting to the West the experience gained through blood and suffering, or even of disturbing the euphoria and complacency that dominate American political science. I might just as well not have hurried, for we are on the threshold of events which will themselves irrefutably convince the West of its own miscalculations.